Praise for *Finding Peace in Tir*

"An insightful and beautiful book th; practical and powerful guide to inner he

—**Carol-Ann Swatling**, abuse and rape survivor, BS in Business Administration, faculty Research and Education Division of the UNLV Libraries.

"Thirty-three long years ago, my husband was killed in an accident, leaving me with four small children to raise alone. I went to see a counselor once, and that was the extent of 'healing' help we had.

"Recently, I read Christy's book and was thunder struck! Over and over again I thought 'Yes! That is exactly how I felt.' and 'Yes! I'm sure my children felt something like this.' I wish I had known some of these healing techniques 33 years ago. It was eye-opening, for me, to see how our brain reacts to trauma and tragedy, and to see how other people feel, helps me to feel freer—like I'm not weird or alone in how I felt and still feel sometimes.

"The healing processes in the book are *extremely* helpful, and simple to follow. I fully intend to utilize and work through these. This book will become a well-used workbook for me, and hopefully my children."

—**Michele McKinnon**, widow for over 30 years, an accountant, writer, and author, *Tales from Two-Bits Street and Beyond*, *Tales from the Wasatch and Beyond*, and *Tales from Ogden Canyon and Beyond*.

"As a brain tumor survivor, this book is my go-to guide for dealing with the on-going effects of trauma. *Finding Peace in Times of Tragedy* masterfully equips the reader with tools to emerge from tragedy and embrace a lifetime of peace. I employ these strategies in my personal life, my writing, and my business."

—**Jodi Orgill Brown**, brain tumor survivor, MS in Organizational Communication, professional speaker, trainer, and author of *The Sun Still Shines*.

"Christy Monson has created an invaluable resource in her book, *Finding Peace in Times of Tragedy*. Full of easy-to-understand steps for healing and peace, along with true stories and examples, this book can help each of us as we navigate through the troubled waters of our time. I highly recommend it."

—**Margot Hovley**, cancer survivor, musician, staff writer for *Ensign Magazine*, and author of *The End Begins* series.

"Christy Monson's skills as a therapist are unmatched. Her talent of deep understanding and sincere love of people qualify her as top in her field."

—**Emma Lu Draper**, English teacher, "Writer As An Advocate for Hope," and blogger at thisandthat3165.blogspot.com.

"Not only is this book a powerful tool for those trying to discover and heal some of the deeply rooted causes of an eating disorder, but it can help prevent some individuals from falling victim to using disordered eating and other addictions as coping mechanisms because they will find true healing within this book instead."

—**Haley Hatch Freeman**, professional speaker and author of *A Future for Tomorrow* and *From Head to Tummy*.

"*Finding Peace in Times of Tragedy* is enlightening, comforting, and answered many questions I had about recovering from trauma. A lot of great techniques and examples of healing are found in this book. Those who read it will find answers to their life's questions and they will know they are not alone in their grief."

—**K Taylor**, young adult, university student.

Finding Peace
IN TIMES OF
Tragedy

Published by Familius LLC, www.familius.com

Familius books are available at special discounts for bulk purchases, whether for sales promotions or for family or corporate use. For more information, contact Familius Sales at 559-876-2170 or email orders@familius.com.

This book is for educational purposes only. It is not a substitute for services from a licensed mental health professional. Should you have personal issues or problems for which you are seeking help, please consult a licensed mental health professional.

Library of Congress Cataloging-in-Publication Data
LCCN 2018956995

Print ISBN 9781641701228
Ebook ISBN 9781641701341

Printed in the United States of America

Edited by Lindsay Sandberg and Nichole Kraft
Cover design by David Miles
Book design by Amanda Clark

10 9 8 7 6 5 4 3 2 1

First Edition

Finding Peace

IN TIMES OF

Tragedy

THE KEYS TO
PEACE AND JOY
WHEN FACING CRISIS

CHRISTY MONSON, LMFT

To all those who suffer from tragedy and loss.

Contents

PART 1

Tragedy—What It Does to Us

The Working World, 9/11 Survivor
Marissa

The Sunday before 9/11, I took my husband's family to look around the towers. I showed them the area. I have a picture of my son there. Of course, he's too little to know what happened, but I have that record—that memory.

I went to work earlier than usual, at 5:30 a.m., on September 11, 2001, because my daughter—who was in high school—had a dental appointment later that day. I'm so happy I did, because I would have been severely affected if I had come to work at 8:30 a.m. as usual.

While I was at work, the building began to shake. At first, I thought it was a helicopter. Then, the windows began shaking. I looked out the windows with a coworker and could see a plane. It was a big Boeing 767. I could see the people through the windows of the airplane just before it flew into the first tower.

I stood frozen, shocked. It's funny how your brain works: I saw the people in the plane. They looked at me, and I looked at them. I saw them—I was the last thing they saw. The plane flew into the building and everything was on fire and smoking, and all I could think about were the people in the plane.

Everyone began looking out the windows. I went back to work at my desk and started typing. It was like it just didn't happen. I couldn't believe it.

Others were asking me questions about the plane. "Was it a little plane?"

"No," I said. "It was a —— 767!" I couldn't believe what just happened.

At that very moment, the phone rang. I answered it. It was a coworker from London.

"What just happened?" he asked.

(I work in commodities on Wall Street, so we have minute-by-minute world news available to us.)

"What the —— was that?" he asked again.

I stood unbelieving—frozen—before I told him.

Everyone was at the windows now.

It was like I had been in a fog. I snapped out of it and called home and told my in-laws, who were taking care of my baby, to put on the news. I hung up.

People all around me were crying. Some men were just staring. We watched people from the first tower holding hands and jumping out of the building to get away from being burned up. I wished there was someone to catch them at the bottom, but there wasn't. People were falling.

My husband called me. "Get out of there," he said. I started to tell him what was happening. He yelled at me to get away from the window and quit watching.

I stood, paralyzed, before I turned away and snapped out of it again. I began to pray and grabbed my bag. "I've got a baby and a teenager," I announced to no one in particular. "I have to go. I'm leaving."

Everyone just stood around in shock. They were not moving.

"I have to go," I said to my coworker.

I opened the door and stood—again frozen—trying to decide whether to take the stairs. I knew that the stairs would be safer. Just at that moment, the elevator door in front of me opened with some of my friends from the floor above.

"Get in," my friends said.

I crowded into the elevator and prayed quietly the whole way down. Afterward, I thought about what an incredibly stupid idea it was to get in the elevator—but at a time like that, you're not thinking.

When we got to the bottom of the building, I ran outside, forgetting that I was in a suit and high heels.

People were standing around watching, like it was a show or something. I couldn't believe it.

My flight response had kicked in. Instinctively, I knew I needed to stay near the water. I headed toward the East River. I knew I could jump in the water and be okay and get home.

About this time, a plane hit the second tower. People were running every which way now. I could have gone several directions, but I decided

I had to get across the Brooklyn Bridge. No cars were moving at this time. People were just running.

I am a runner, so it was second nature for me to run. I didn't take notice of my heels or my suit. I just ran, covered in dust and looking to survive. On the bridge was a woman with a baby in a front pack. She was running with a purpose: to get her baby safe on the other side. I kept praying. The Brooklyn Bridge is a mile-long landmark, and it could have been a target as well. I had to get across.

When I got to the other side of the bridge, I realized I was still in my heels. I went into a store to buy some cheap sneakers, but I didn't have any cash, and all the banks were closed. I couldn't use my card. The clerk just looked at me and gave me the shoes. I guess I looked like I needed them, covered in dust from the destruction. I thanked her.

I walked down the street. No one's cell phones worked, and there were long lines to use the few pay phones available. I remembered that when I was growing up there were always phones in the laundromats. So, I hunted until I came to a laundromat.

I called my mother. Up to this time, I had been under control. But when I heard my mother on the other end of the phone, my voice cracked. I wanted to cry. My mother heard it and wanted me to stay strong so I could get home. She made a joke and then another joke. It caught me off guard, and I managed to get myself together, stuffing the panic deep inside. She told me to go to my aunt's house, who lived in Brooklyn.

I had no idea how I would do that. Everything was shut down.

When I left, I walked into a bar to find out what was happening.

Someone offered me a drink, but I had no money. They told me, "Your money isn't good here." They gave me the drink anyway.

People were so kind and generous. I saw the TVs turned to the news and I began to think about all my colleagues.

Someone asked me, "Are you okay?"

I put my head down on the table and cried.

I was starving and needed to eat. I had only a dollar in my purse, but they wouldn't take even that. When I had my food, a lady asked me where I was from.

I told her, "Jersey."

"That's where I'm from," she said. She told me she would take me home. In that moment of crisis, I trusted a perfect stranger and went with her. She was a nice lady. It took us a long time to get to New Jersey. The roads were all crowded and some of them were closed. None of the tollbooths worked—we just went right on through. Everything was shut down. We got to her place in South Jersey, but I lived in North Jersey. This lady had been so nice to bring me this far. She was so thankful to be safe and with her family. It would have been an imposition for her to take me all the way. I called my sister to come and get me.

Finally, my sister came to get me. I got home about 10:00 that night. My husband got home about the same time. He had been in another area of New York. My in-laws were there with my children. We were home together and safe.

When I went to bed, I could hear airplanes all night long. I knew there were no planes outside. The noise was inside my head. (After that day, I cringed every time I heard an airplane. One night, I was making dinner and just scraping a plate of scraps into the garbage. I heard an airplane fly by. I cringed and ducked. After, I looked around to see if anyone saw me. I was embarrassed. There were times like that when I just froze. I tried to put it in the back of my mind.)

I had a friend who called me the next day. He was on vacation. He's the kind of person who loves to save the world. I told him, "I know if you had been here, I would have gone with you to help you save everyone, and we would have died."

I have another friend whose husband had had a mini stroke. She wasn't there at work that day. I told her, "I was glad you were gone because if you'd been there I would have had to carry you across the bridge, and I couldn't have done that. We would have died."

It was a blessing that those two friends weren't there that day.

I wanted to go right back to work. I wanted things to be back to normal. So the next day, I called my boss and asked, "What can I do?"

I could have gone to the support groups and talked about things, but I needed to be busy again. I didn't want to just focus on myself and be depressed. I cried in quiet moments—alone—in the shower.

I went to work right away. The company took only a few people back. We had an office in New Jersey—on the thirty-third floor. The first day, I stood at the bottom of the building and remembered looking up and thinking: *Really! All the way up there?*

My boss asked me who I wanted to work with. I chose a few good people. I knew the customers. I knew who was honest and who would be cheaters. Because of 9/11, some of the people thought they could get away with not calling the margins, but we kept everything honest.

Soon, we were back in New York.

As the weeks went by, I had to go to my favorite places in New York to make sure everything was okay. It was like checking in to see if things were still there. I went to the Metropolitan Museum of Art. After I spent some time in the museum, I went into the restaurant to have a cup of coffee. I just sat for a long time and looked out the window, thinking about things. I was so absorbed, I didn't notice that there was an artist there with his girlfriend, sitting at a close table. He sketched a picture of me because he could tell I was deep in thought. He gave me the picture, and it means a lot to me.

This whole tragedy was an eye-opener for me. I tell my family how much I love them now. Life is fragile. You never know how long you'll be here. I value everyone more. I say thank you more. I apologize more.

To this day, I cannot look at any documentary on 9/11. Every year, I think I'm over it . . . and I try to be, but I can't. And just talking about it makes me realize how weak I really am . . . because it breaks my heart.

In retrospect, I know that there were blessings, even in the midst of something so awful:

- A picture with my infant son at the trade towers two days before the tragedy.
- My husband's phone call to get out.
- The elevator door opening in front of me with my friends on it.
- A pair of sneakers from a store clerk when I had no money.
- A laundromat pay phone.
- My mother's jokes.
- Food and drink from people I didn't know.
- A ride to Jersey.
- I know that life is fragile. I know we can be here today and gone tomorrow.

CHAPTER 1

Personal Tragedy

A father is a daughter's first love.
—Author Unknown

I stood on the sidewalk of the school—just outside my first grade class-room, watching for my mother and little brother to turn the corner and walk up the street. They didn't come. My hands felt cold and clammy. My stomach did a flip-flop.

"Where's your mother today?" asked my teacher. "She's usually here on the dot."

My mouth felt dry. "I—I don't know."

"Well," said my teacher, "she'll be here soon."

But she wasn't. Everyone else left. I was alone.

Something was wrong. I tried to swallow the tears. I was a big girl—six years old. I shouldn't cry. My mother would be here. She wouldn't forget.

All of a sudden, our neighbor, Mrs. Jones, sped around the corner in her car. She pulled up to the curb. "I'm so sorry," she said through her tears.

What was wrong? I shivered.

Mrs. Jones ran to my teacher and threw her arms around her, saying something I couldn't hear.

My teacher's face grew white, and she shook her head and covered her mouth. She rushed over to put her arms around me. Tears welled up in her eyes. "I'm so sorry. I'm so sorry," she kept repeating.

Fear filled me. What was happening?

Mrs. Jones put her arms around me and ushered me into the car.

"What's the matter?" I asked.

She didn't answer but began to cry all over again.

It must be terrible, I thought. *No one is talking.*

We pulled up to the house. A police car parked in the driveway behind my grandfather's car. Grandpa lived far away. Why did he come?

Mrs. Jones helped me out of the car and put her hand on my back. She rushed me into the house. My mother, who was talking to the policeman, thanked her and pulled me close to her.

Something was very sad. I looked up at her, and she burst into tears but didn't say anything. The policeman continued speaking to her.

I felt confused and angry. Why wasn't someone telling me what happened?

My little brother ran his fire truck back and forth under the dining room table. He had no idea what was going on either.

I have a vivid memory of feeling afraid and looking at the lower halves of the people in the room. It was like a bad dream—a nightmare. No one said anything to me.

I caught snatches of conversations. "Angry teenager . . . driving at high speed . . . ran a stop sign . . . hit the car broadside . . . farmer said the car knocked into the air . . . as high as the telephone pole . . . killed instantly . . . new Buick demolished."

My father had just bought a new Buick—a large car to keep him safe.

I didn't know what *broadside* or *demolished* meant. But I figured it out from the rest. My father was dead—killed in a car crash.

I felt jumbled inside. I ran to my room and curled up on my bed with my blanket. My dad was dead. I had so many questions. I would ask him all about it when he put me to bed tonight.

I waited, but he didn't come home.

I looked for my dad to drive in the driveway, but he never came.

My mother cried and cried. I didn't want her to leave too. I was afraid, but I didn't cry. I had to be strong for her. If I smiled, I could make her smile. I felt myself shutting off on the inside—sadness locked away.

We ate supper, and my grandpa rocked me to sleep.

That night and in nights to come, I dreamed about my dad. I dreamed about the times we snacked on cheese and crackers at the kitchen table and told each other jokes. I dreamed about him rubbing my back before I went to sleep. I dreamed about our walks with the dog—and his laugh. I dreamed about him holding me close.

As time went by, my mother was still so sad, and I kept my feelings deep inside. I tried not to let them show. At night before I slipped off to sleep, I pictured my dad putting me to bed, reading to me, and singing to me. I could tell him anything.

I continued this practice of picturing him there and talking things over with him into my early adult life. Even now, when I am stressed, my dad and I discuss my problems.

Those locked-away feelings surface at times—private times. No one ever sees them but me. I make sure of that—it's not safe. I have to make sure others are happy.

Several months after the accident, the young man who had killed my father came to the house with his father to apologize. He was dressed in rumpled work clothes. He needed a haircut, and I could see yellow earwax coming from his ears. His words were clipped and seemed forced. I sat politely and listened to him because my mother made me come into the room. I suspect that young man didn't want to be there any more than I did.

This tragedy happened over sixty years ago, and I traveled many miles before letting my fear, grief, and anxiety go. As a child, I didn't understand what had happened. I knew the words, but I didn't understand them. I expected my father to walk through the door that night even when I knew he was dead.

My mother's emotions continued to brim over during those first few years after the accident. My father was the one and only true love of her life. She remained single for sixty years until she died, waiting to rejoin him in heaven. I never did share my feelings with her. I always tried to make sure she was happy—to protect her.

The irony of the situation was that my father had been gone for the first four years of my life. World War II was raging, and he was stationed in Egypt in military intelligence, decoding German messages for the Army. While there, he contracted diphtheria and almost died.

He came home with a severely damaged heart. He wouldn't have lived long anyway.

I had just gotten acquainted with him when he died, making my little-girl sadness even greater.

My mother and my grandparents loved me, but it wasn't the same as having my dad there.

As I grew up, I felt awkward around boys. I shied away from social activities as a teenager. I didn't know how to act around men.

In my later grade-school years, Mother talked about the accident briefly so I knew the details. My father, the county agent of Minidoka County, Idaho, drove his new Buick along the country roads, enjoying the warm sunshine of October. He had just been to visit a farm and was heading home.

Another car barreled toward him on a crossroad at a high speed, ran a stop sign, and hit my father's Buick broadside. The collision sent my father's car into the air "almost as high as the telephone pole," the farmer in the nearby field reported.

My father was killed instantly—the teenage driver, angry at his dad because he didn't want to dig potatoes, walked away from the accident unharmed.

This tragedy would affect my family and change my life drastically. Things would never be the same.

Mother locked the pictures of the smashed car, the keys, my dad's sun glasses, and a few other items in a small portable safe. She told my brother and I to leave it closed until her death.

It was a horrible accident locked away—not to be seen or discussed.

I closed myself off emotionally. I had been abandoned—happiness ripped away from me, as I saw it. I felt afraid. I was angry, but I couldn't show it. It wasn't safe.

My mother and I became best friends as life progressed. We could talk about anything—except the accident. That was a subject we never broached. There was too much hurt and sadness associated with it for both of us. She was always so concerned whenever my husband and I traveled anywhere. I always had to call her and tell her I was okay.

As I grew up, I pictured myself close to my dad. At night when I went to bed, I would feel him near, reading me stories like he used to do. It comforted me. If I had a question about life, I would talk things over with him. I wrote my memories of him in a journal as I grew older. My mother and I never talked about him, but I always kept his memory near me.

It wasn't until I started studying psychology that I was able to work through the grief, though my dream conversations with him helped me cope for years.

Whenever I see a news item of a young policeman, soldier, or workman who dies, I always wonder if they have left small children. Sadness tugs at my heart. I know the road those children will walk.

This tragedy was the first in my life. As time went along, I experienced the birth of a premature baby weighing just over a pound, grieved the loss of several loved ones to cancer and then death, and learned to set healthy boundaries in an extended alcoholic family.

In my counseling practice in Las Vegas, I worked with countless others whose tragedies include date rape, childhood sexual abuse, battery, death of a spouse by murder, death of spouse in an experimental plane crash, and survivors of horrors like the Nazi death camps and ritualistic abuse. No matter the specific tragedy, trauma affects us all.

What is the path to healing? How do we get beyond tragedy to make life as normal as we can? Is the grief ever really gone?

The answer to these questions will vary for each of us as we read the following pages. No matter your own experience, this book has tools that can help you understand the hidden grief, hurt, and sadness inside you and find your path toward peace and healing.

CHAPTER 2

Symptoms and Feelings We Experience When Tragedy Strikes

I thought I could describe a state; make a map of sorrow. Sorrow, however, turns out to be not a state but a process.
—C. S. Lewis, *A Grief Observed*

The world is full of tragedies these days. They have become commonplace in our news.

Worldwide traumas are all around us today. As we hear the news, we vicariously experience these tragedies: terrorist attacks leaving many wounded and dead; earthquakes, hurricanes, tornadoes, and other natural disasters stripping thousands of their homes and protection from the elements without food and water; abductions keeping us all on the alert to protect our families; and countless monstrosities too numerous to name.

We may experience many physical, mental, and emotional symptoms when we are confronted with a disaster. Even if we aren't directly involved in newsworthy world calamities, they still affect our lives. I just finished reading Stephen E. Ambrose's *Undaunted Courage*, a book about the Lewis and Clark Expedition to the Northwest. Meriwether Lewis brings his life to a close by committing suicide. As I read these last pages of the book, I felt a deep sadness over this incident. My sympathy extended to Thomas Jefferson, his mentor; to his lifelong friend William Clark; and to his mother. This incident happened over two hundred years ago, and yet I was grieving for this loss of life. This man made a great contribution to the United States of America as we know it today.

Tragedy has a ripple effect. Like the dropping of a pebble in a still pond, the waves spread ever outward, enveloping us all.

Personal trauma belongs to all our lives, and these situations affect us even more deeply.

Sometimes our trials manifest as the death of a child or the loss of a spouse. Everyone knows about them. For others, sadness and misfortune is internal in the quiet places of the heart, like sexual abuse or secret addictions of family members that remain unknown to those around us. Whatever your situation is, there is healing through light and love.

My hope is that you can use this book as a tool to discover the strengths and weaknesses in your experiences, as you see them. Acknowledge that they are part of your existence. Writing out your feelings and articulating your experience is proven as beneficial to the healing process. With the guidance in this book, you can choose the path to healing that best fits you. James Pennebaker of the University of Texas at Austin, found that those who wrote about their experience after a tragedy had better health. They went to the doctor less, felt happier, and let go of anxiety and depression more quickly than those who didn't write.

Use the commitment goals at the end of each chapter to lead you toward personal healing. The emotional toll of surviving tragedy can be devastating. When we experience tragedy, often symptoms of anxiety come to the forefront. Feelings of depression can follow.

Symptoms of Anxiety

Jane walked into my office wanting to deal with the emotional turmoil of having hit a person with her car in a parking lot. Her face looked tight—full of tension. She closed and opened her hands, twisting her fingers at times. She sat back in her chair as we started the interview, but as she began explaining the circumstances surrounding the accident, she leaned forward, crossing and uncrossing her legs. She had a difficult time maintaining her composure as she talked.

Assess your symptoms in relationship to your own tragedy with the following charts. Take an honest inventory of your feelings at the time of the trauma. Make another record of your feelings at the present time. Can you see the areas that have changed? What has that process been like for you? There are many gifts that come from tragedy. It leads all of us to feel empathy for others. But first we must get outside our own feelings, look at them for what they are, understand the meaning they bring to our lives, and grow from the experience.

How I felt right after the accident:

_____ A state of shock

_____ Trembling or shaking uncontrollably (hands, arms, legs, or entire body)

_____ Racing heart (pounding until you feel you are going to explode)

_____ Choking sensations (feeling unable to catch your breath)

_____ Rapid breathing

_____ Nausea or vomiting

_____ Dizziness, feeling faint

_____ Fatigue

_____ Tense muscles

_____ Excessive worry

_____ Agitation

_____ Inability to sleep

    _____ Inability to fall asleep

    _____ Inability to stay asleep

_____ Nightmares

_____ Racing thoughts

_____ Confusion

Experiencing these symptoms can cause you to feel like you're having a heart attack. Check with a doctor to make sure your heart is functioning properly. I have had clients come to me, worrying that their hearts were malfunctioning when really they were experiencing panic. Both need to be treated, so check with your doctor to be sure of your health.

How I feel today:

_____ A state of shock

_____ Trembling or shaking uncontrollably (hands, arms, legs, or entire body)

_____ Racing heart (pounding until you feel you are going to explode)

_____ Choking sensations (feeling unable to catch your breath)

_____ Rapid breathing

_____ Nausea or vomiting

_____ Dizziness, feeling faint

_____ Fatigue

Tense muscles

_____ Excessive worry

_____ Agitation

_____ Inability to sleep

    _____ Inability to fall asleep

    _____ Inability to stay asleep

_____ Nightmares

_____ Racing thoughts

_____ Confusion

What has this process of change been like for you?

_____

_____

_____

_____

_____

Symptoms of Depression

Depression can be present alone without anxiety. As the weeks and months pile up after the loss of a loved one, we realize our hurt is permanent. I finally figured out that my father wasn't coming back, and though I didn't recognize it at the time, symptoms of depression settled in me. I felt I had a knot in my stomach all the time. I withdrew into myself. I had a hard time laughing and having fun. Life became very serious to me.

How I felt right after the accident:

_____ Depressed mood

_____ Irritability

_____ Decreased interest or pleasure in life

_____ Significant weight changes

_____ Changes in sleep patterns

_____ Changes in activity

    _____ Agitation

    _____ Lethargy

_____ Loss of energy

_____ Feelings of guilt

_____ Feelings of worthlessness

_____ Inability to concentrate

_____ Suicidal ideation

How I feel today:

_____ Depressed mood

_____ Irritability

_____ Decreased interest or pleasure in life

_____ Significant weight changes

_____ Changes in sleep patterns

_____ Changes in activity

    _____ Agitation

    _____ Lethargy

_____ Loss of energy

_____ Feelings of guilt

_____ Feelings of worthlessness
_____ Inability to concentrate
_____ Suicidal ideation

What has this process of change been like for you?

_____

_____

_____

_____

When these symptoms are present, it is an effort to even get out of bed. Daily life requires an overwhelming effort. If many of these indicators are present, see a doctor for medical help and find a good therapist. While this book contains many wonderful and helpful coping tools, it is wise to work with professionals who can give you immediate support.

Summary

Use the checklists above as a guide to help you identify your feelings and begin your healing process. The words in the lists may not be quite right to identify the feelings. If that's the case, change the words to match your inner experience. Add to the list if you have other feelings to work through. Modify the list to fit your individual struggle. Take the time throughout the book to personalize the healing process to meet your needs.

Commitment

- Take an honest inventory of your feelings right after the accident.
- Take an honest inventory of your feelings today.
- What stages of grief have you experienced in the past?
- What stages are you experiencing today?

CHAPTER 3

Healing Is a Process

The emotion that can break your heart is sometimes the very one that heals it . . .
—Nicholas Sparks, *At First Sight*

Healing is a process. In my practice in Las Vegas, I worked with people who had experienced many forms of trauma—from the horrors of World War II to sexual abuse, from spousal attacks to witnessing murder. Their journey of recovery took time. It didn't happen in just a few therapy sessions; it became a course of learning a new way to walk with peace and light.

Immediately after a traumatic incident, we are in a state of shock. Fear may overwhelm us. Many times, the trauma involves death of people we know—friends and family. When this happens, there are several stages we go through.

James was devastated when his teenage son was killed in a car accident as he was coming home from football practice. First, denial set in. *This can't really be happening. This is worse than a nightmare*, he thought. His immediate physical response was to crouch—hunched back, arms protecting his chest, head down, and legs bent. He wanted to curl up in a corner in the fetal position to protect himself and isolate his heart and mind from the knowledge that his son was gone. James felt guilt that he didn't drive his son to practice that day, that he survived and his son didn't.

Anger then reared its head. "How can this be happening to me? To my family? What did I do to deserve this? It's so unfair," James ranted, angry at God. How could He let this happen?

As the anger receded, James tried to bargain with God. "If you will just help me through this, if you bring him back, I'll . . ."

Shame dogged James whenever he was around others. And in the face of such loss, many people felt awkward around James. They didn't know what to say. The awkwardness and shame made James uncomfortable, even with the briefest interactions. *What do they think of me? Will they judge me because this happened?* he wondered.

Depression became a regular challenge for James, impairing his ability to focus on work or find comfort in his remaining children and wife. *It's so unfair*, he thought. *Why did this happen to my son?*

But as time went on and James sought support from family and friends, he began to heal. As the denial, anger, bargaining, shame, and depression receded, relief and acceptance could come into his heart and mind.

As you read this, you could be anywhere or at any stage. So where to begin? Relief and acceptance seem a world away right now.

At times, we experience these stages in the order they are listed. At other times, we float back and forth through several of them over and over again.

Stages of Grief

How I felt right after the accident:

_____ Denial

_____ Anger

_____ Bargaining

_____ Shame

_____ Depression

_____ Acceptance

How I feel now:

_____ Denial

_____ Anger

_____ Bargaining

_____ Shame

_____ Depression

_____ Acceptance

What has this process of change been like for you?

_____

_____

_____

_____

After a traumatic event, these stages are signs and your body's way of saying, "Help, I'm in trouble right now! Listen to me. Hear my anguish."

I have had clients tell me they feel like they are in a deep, dark hole with no way out. This mind-set creates more depression and anxiety.

After my father died, I hid in my bedroom—but beyond that, I hid inside myself, wondering if I would ever come out.

So what is the answer? How do we climb out of this deep, dark hole? How do we find peace amid all these problems? Where is our hope? How do we go on?

Summary

Right after tragedy happens to us, we live with symptoms of anxiety and depression. Sometimes, we move through these feelings and can let them go. At other times, they are part of our existence. We are unable to move beyond our personal trauma.

There are universal stages of grief we go through: denial, anger, bargaining, shame, depression, and acceptance.

People emote in very different ways. Some may not need to cry. Others dissolve in tears. Grief is something many need to talk about. Others prefer to work it out in the privacy of their own being. Lots of people need a physical release. Others don't. Give yourself permission to do things your way. Don't feel like you're doing it wrong if you're not like your neighbor.

Commitment

- Take an honest inventory of your feelings right after the accident.
- Take an honest inventory of your feelings today.
- What stages of grief have you experienced in the past?
- What stages are you experiencing today?

CHAPTER 4

Tragedy and the Brain

Turn your wounds into wisdom.
—Oprah Winfrey

When we experience a tragedy, our mental and physical well-being is disrupted. The entire body, including the brain, becomes unsettled. Michele Rosenthal reports in *Heal Your PTSD: Dynamic Strategies That Work*: "After any type of trauma (from combat to car accidents, natural disasters to domestic violence, sexual assault to child abuse), the brain and body change. Every cell records memories and every embedded, trauma-related neuropathway has the opportunity to repeatedly reactivate."

The traumatic memory is stored in every cell of our person. Christy Matta, in *The Stress Response*, claims: "Parts of the brain can become sensitized, causing you to be on high alert and to perceive threats all around, leaving you jumpy and anxious."

Information about the catastrophe floods the emotional areas of the brain, avoiding the sections that process reason, thinking, and understanding. For some people, these changes are only temporary and last a short time; but for others of us, these recorded emotional impairments can continue to bombard us, interfering with our work, our associations, and our family.

It is difficult for survivors to understand that physical changes have occurred that deeply effect their lives. The recovery process should start with an understanding of the result tragedy has on the brain and the symptoms that follow these changes.

Post-traumatic stress disorder (PTSD) is a frightening place to get stuck. Friends may tell you to "get over it," but your physical body, including your brain, has changed. You can't just get over it.

PTSD brings with it invasive thoughts and memories, unexpected changes in mood, hypervigilance, startled responses, and a tendency to hide away like I did—especially from all trauma-related issues.

Any or all of the symptoms of anxiety and depression can be present. As one of my clients put it, "My life just isn't my own anymore. I don't know who I am now."

I have a dear friend, Venice, who experienced abuse and neglect during her early childhood. Her father was a kind and gentle person when he was not drinking; but if he went on a binge, he would turn into a raging drunk. Venice lived in fear, even when her father was sober, because she never knew when the next binge was coming. Growing up, she felt worthless—beneath the other kids. Shame clung to her like a shroud.

One day, we went to lunch, and I began to tell Venice about the effects abuse and trauma had on the brain.

When she heard this, a light came into her eyes. "You mean there have been chemical changes in my brain that cause me to get so emotional? All my life, I have felt flawed. I don't have to carry this cloud of darkness anymore?"

I encouraged her to read more about how the brain changes so she could gain greater understanding. Many, if not all, of the abuse survivors I worked with experienced a lot of shame.

Read through the rest of this chapter, even if you don't remember the names of the different parts of the brain. Digest the information here to help you release the shame you carry and realize your brain is reacting to stored memories. As you work through these issues with the techniques outlined in this book, you can release them and come to live a more peaceful life.

When we have experienced tragedy, brain scans show that the thinking side of the brain in the left frontal cortex freezes or shuts down. But the right hemisphere lights with activity, keeping pictures and the emotions of the trauma.

Three sections of the brain play an active role in triggering trauma-related symptoms in those who have been exposed to disaster. These sections change physically when exposed to trauma and continue to trigger fear and stress symptoms long after the disturbance is over.

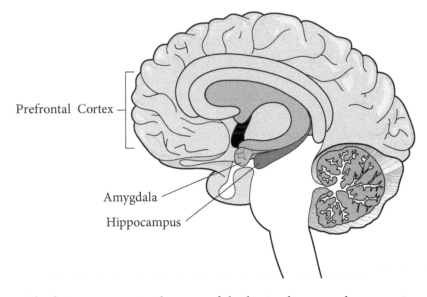

The **hippocampus** is the part of the brain that records memories. After a traumatic event, this area of the brain becomes smaller because the event triggers an increase of the stress hormone glucocorticoid, which kills hippocampus cells. The hippocampus is, therefore, less effective in helping us remember events or call to mind things that happened in the past. Because of this, many PTSD clients are not able to distinguish between the past and the present. They are confused as to what happened before and what's happening right now.

For Venice, this meant that she lived in fear of her father's abuse even when he was kind. She always waited for the other shoe to drop. She didn't notice the good times because she was afraid of the bad. As a child, she didn't grasp the fact that his drinking brought on the rages. When she was little, she couldn't understand why she had a raging father and the other kids didn't. She reasoned that she must not be as good as the children who had kind fathers. She felt ashamed of her family. Her memories were distorted.

The **amygdala** is the section of the brain that helps us process emotions, including fear. After a traumatic incident, it kicks into alert mode, looking for and finding perceived threats at every turn. Brain scans show that PTSD clients have an overly active amygdala when exposed to pictures or events associated with the trauma or abuse. Even if they just see a picture of a disturbance, they become afraid. Fear may take over even in situations not associated with the trauma.

As Venice grew older, she never associated with people who drank. She became hypersensitive to associates who had a temper or exhibited any anger at all. She married a very gentle, kind man who never raised his voice.

The **ventromedial prefrontal cortex** is supposed to regulate the emotional responses of the amygdala. When someone experiences a calamity, this section of the brain becomes smaller and doesn't work as well as it did before the trauma. So when PTSD clients are exposed to stressful situations—even those not associated with the specific trauma—their fear, anxiety, and stress are allowed to run wild.

With this in mind, it isn't surprising that when the less active hippocampus and the under-functioning ventromedial prefrontal cortex can't do their jobs, the amygdala can go into extreme-stress mode, causing heightened anxiety.

Venice still experiences anxiety when she is with a group of people. She has a hard time with anyone who is outspoken at all. She learned, over the years, to avoid situations that caused her anxiety and learned to lose herself in her music. "My piano is my therapy," she says.

This may look like a bleak picture, but the body and brain have an innate ability to regenerate themselves. With time and help, the damaging process can be reversed. The amygdala can learn to calm itself down. The hippocampus can regain its ability to process memory, and the ventromedial prefrontal cortex can again regulate emotional responses.

Do any of these symptoms seem familiar?
- Flashbacks of the trauma
- A feeling of reliving the trauma
- Dreams/nightmares of the trauma
- Avoidance of objects associated with the trauma

- Avoidance of thoughts or associations with the trauma
- Experiencing negative thoughts about yourself
- Difficulty experiencing positive emotions
- Memory problems
- Inability to maintain close relationships
- Feeling detached from friends and family

Healing is as varied as are those who experience tragedy. Many of the examples in this book are clients I worked with. Several stories, however, including my own, happened many years before therapeutic techniques and understanding of the brain were developed. These people discovered the general principles of healing or coping on their own and walked beyond personal tragedy by themselves.

Some wellness practices are common in the lives of survivors who work through personal disaster and remain highly functioning, as we will see. If a person is willing to explore and be open to new healing techniques, the effects of trauma and symptoms of PTSD can be reduced and even eliminated.

Summary

Traumatic events affect the brain and its chemistry. Research shows this process is not just in our imagination. Tragedy causes real changes in us. Those who suffer from PTSD have a difficult time controlling their emotions when confronted with memories of their trauma. Techniques and insights in the following pages will give insight to the path of healing and peace.

Commitment
- Record your feelings about this section.
- Now that you know that tragedy causes physiological changes in the brain, does that change your thinking about trauma?
- Does it help validate your feelings?

CHAPTER 5

Tragedy and the Body

The gem cannot be polished without friction,
nor a man perfected without trials.

—Confucius

The body reacts to trauma as well as the brain. Both the body and brain work together in a complex interactive system. All of our sensory experiences cause electrochemical reactions in our entire being. Our brain releases chemicals that send information to the rest of our body—including our nervous system—and then messages are sent back to the brain. This constant sequence triggers our reactions to things, including our movements and thoughts. Much of this happens automatically, so that we are not aware of it. It's the same response as if we come in contact with a hot stove and we immediately pull our hands back without thinking.

The autonomic nervous system has two parts: (1) the sympathetic, and (2) the parasympathetic. The sympathetic nervous system kicks in with the fight-or-flight response. Think back to the time you became aware of the tragedy happening in your life. Did you want to fight or flee?

A neighbor lady up the street from our home has five little yappy schnauzers. Whenever they are out in the yard, they bark up a storm when I go by on my daily walk. One afternoon as I walked by, the lady was outside with only three of the dogs. I asked her where the others were. With tears in her eyes, she told me they had been poisoned. As she vented her rage, she became obviously angry, battling the urge to fight. How could someone poison innocent puppies? It was a visceral experience for her—arms flinging out and head tipping up and down. How about you? Call to mind a fight-or-flight incident in your life. Can you feel the muscle tension associated with it? We will explore incidents of body memories in later chapters.

The parasympathetic nervous system controls the freeze response. In the grocery store the other day, I witnessed a father yell at his little girl to "quit climbing on the cart!" She froze, ducked her head, and climbed down. That little child stored that frozen response in her body. For many people, even after the incident is over, that frozen response gives way to anger. For that little girl, will it turn into anger toward herself? Toward others? We can't answer that, but we do know the feelings will be recorded in her brain and her body.

How about you? Recall a time when you froze. Can you still feel it in your body or is it only a memory now?

These two systems (sympathetic and parasympathetic) synchronize the body's emotions and physiological functions. During our normal day, these systems can be activated if anything happens and then return to status quo after the problem is past. But if tragedy occurs or we are exposed to ongoing stress, these systems can become activated and essentially malfunction, causing us to move into a state of anxiety and panic (sympathetic) or send us into a nonresponsive state (parasympathetic).

Either way, the body has recorded the tragedy and responded to it, so the memory is documented in our body as well as our brain. As we consider recovery plans, we must include body-healing techniques as well.

Throughout the book, I will emphasize body work along with emotional healing. Many of my clients included workouts and external body activity such as yoga, massage therapy, and other curative techniques as part of their wellness program. We must also include the creative arts: dance, music, painting, and other creative ventures can also involve large-muscle activities. They are valuable methods of healing because they not only access the memories stored in our physical bodies but they also open the door to the emotional side of our brains for comprehensive healing.

It's important for everyone to engage in body work that fits their symptoms. For instance, if a person is struggling to overcome the trauma of abuse or other situations of powerlessness, it's helpful for them to find large-muscle exercises that will empower them—like aerobic exercise or self-defense classes. If a person is struggling with depression or grief, yoga or massage can enhance self-care skills. It's important for each person to choose what will work for them. There is empowerment in the choice.

A great variety of health-giving techniques are at our fingertips with the explosion of knowledge on the internet. Choose carefully the practices that will work for you. Even though we are alike in many ways, we are also different and must find our own paths to healing.

If you don't know where to start, answer some of these questions to narrow down what body work may help you most.

- Do you feel better after rigorous exercise?
- Do you feel better after meditating or spending time quietly?
- Would you feel safe if someone were massaging your shoulders or restraining you in a self-defense practice?

Best wishes in this process. My only caution for this quest is that you choose techniques that are safe for yourself and others and that are respectful to your body.

In all you do, be kind to yourself.

Summary

The body stores traumatic experiences along with the brain. The sympathetic and parasympathetic nervous systems record these happenings in the tissues and muscles of the body. Body work is as important to healing as mental therapies. There are many techniques to aid wellness, and because of the internet, knowledge is easily accessible to us.

Commitment

- Consider the types of body work that are available to you.
- Study each of them that you think will be healing for you.
- We will discuss this subject in greater depth in later chapters. You can make your decision then.

PART 2

Tragedy and Healing

Two Daughters, the Same Brain Tumors
Jeremy and Colette

Jeremy and I had a young, busy family of six children—the oldest (Jennifer), three boys, another girl (Lucille), and a younger son.

Jennifer was a typical oldest child. She liked to organize things and tell everyone what to do. She was a good student who loved to read. When she was about twelve, she began to have headaches. She seemed to get them only on Sundays. At first, I accused her of not wanting to go to church. But soon, the headaches became more severe, and she had trouble with her eyes.

Since I was a nurse, I chided myself for not believing Jennifer at first. I took her to see an eye doctor. He checked her eyes and said there seemed to be something pressing on her optic nerve. He referred her to a large children's hospital in the nearest metropolitan area.

After a thorough battery of tests, the doctors found a tumor behind Jennifer's eyes. The surgeons operated but couldn't get it all. They gave her large doses of radiation to kill the tumor.

Jennifer's eyesight became worse. She struggled to keep up with her schoolwork the best she could. Her headaches increased, and she was often sick to her stomach. Soon, she was completely blind. We got a braille teacher so Jennifer could continue reading.

Jennifer spent more and more time in the hospital. She began to have seizures. They gave her radiation to shrink the tumor, and that made her even sicker.

I continued to care for our other five children, work, and nurse a sick child. I felt tremendous pressure during that time, and by the end of each day, I was exhausted. Jeremy was good support, but he had a job and all the stresses that went with it.

It's hard to see your child suffer. It would have been easier for me to take the pain and illness myself rather than to see Jennifer endure it like she did. Sometimes I felt despondent.

Jennifer became bedridden.

We tried to keep things as normal as possible so we planned a birthday for her. She felt so sick, we had to call it off.

The braille teacher continued to work with her and became a good friend to the family. Church members helped by bringing meals and assisting with Jennifer's care.

After Jennifer finally passed away, the autopsy showed that many of the nerves and blood vessels in her spinal column were damaged by the radiation.

The boys had a hard time watching their sister die. This entire process took its toll on the whole family. Jeremy and I grieved together, but we still felt empty inside. I don't know what we would have done without each other.

After the funeral, life got back to normal. We were busy with our family of five children now—rather than six.

When our second daughter, Lucille, was about twelve, she began to have headaches. I had a sinking feeling in my stomach.

"It's not true," I told Jeremy. "Lucille doesn't have a tumor like Jennifer had." I took Lucille to the eye doctor.

"It's not the same thing Jennifer had," the eye doctor said. "It couldn't be. The chances of it being the same thing are one in a million."

I still had the sinking feeling. Lucille's headaches continued. I took her to the doctors at the children's hospital where Jennifer had been treated. The staff all agreed it couldn't be the same diagnosis. They ran the tests.

It was.

The doctors were astounded.

I was very cautious this time around. I didn't want Lucille to have too much radiation. Lucille's tumor was operated on and radiated some, but not to the extent that Jennifer's had been.

About this time, I attended a church conference in New York. One of the speakers was a lady with a young child who had suffered from cancer a few years earlier. I went up to talk to her after the meeting.

I clung to every word she said to me about her own tragedy. I hung onto the fact that she had survived the ordeal and was now on the other end of it. I kept thinking, *If she can make it, I can make it.*

The braille teacher, still a family friend, came to teach Lucille and help with her schoolwork.

Lucille had watched Jennifer die. "Am I going to suffer and die like Jennifer?" she asked. Both Jeremy and I agonized over her question. What could we tell her?

Church members rallied around our family again. They came to help when Lucille was bedridden. They brought meals. I don't know what I would have done without the church. I did my own laundry, though. It was mundane work that helped me through my grief.

Lucille's seizures followed the same pattern Jennifer's had. Finally, at the dinner table one evening, Lucille had her last seizure. Her father gently laid her on the floor where she passed away.

The autopsy showed her spinal column was full of cancer. She had not been given enough radiation. The doctor dissolved in tears when she saw the results.

All of our family came for the funeral. Even those who lived around the country made an extra effort to be there.

I don't know how we got through it.

"I was angry at God for a while," Jeremy told me. "But I made a conscious decision to continue in my faith. As I stayed close to my church and served the people, my anger dissipated, and I found my own peace.

"It still hurts. Whenever I see a young bride in a movie or a TV commercial, all of a sudden, the sadness is there. My girls won't have those moments here on earth."

Collette also struggled. I was asked to serve in the girls' youth organization at church. I had to decline. I just couldn't do it. It was too sad for me to be there and see those young girls growing into womanhood. My girls were gone.

But I couldn't think about it like that and keep myself strong. Instead, I look at it this way: the girls are away from home for an extended time. Other people's children go on trips or to college and are absent for a while. My girls and I have a lengthy separation right now. I can visualize them in heaven, together. But I know I will see them again.

There is sadness in our entire family. The boys are all grown now. When they decided to marry, our future daughters-in-law were skeptical about marrying into the family. What if they had little girls? Would their fate be the same as our girls? No one knows the answer to that.

One day, I remarked to one of the boys, "Your little girl reminds me so much of Jennifer."

He turned to me and said, "Mother, don't say that."

My heart sank. I probably don't realize how much the boys suffered through this ordeal. It's left its mark on all of us.

One of the reasons I wanted to tell our story is because others who are going through their own trials will be better for knowing the path we have walked.

I was so grateful for that speaker in New York. I clung to her words of survival. I would like to give the story of our trials to others as a gift. Maybe it will help them like it helped me. Because, despite the tragedy and grief, there were many gifts:

- Our faith increased.
- We have belief in life after this one.
- We grew closer as a couple.
- We learned to receive love.
- We gained spiritual and emotional strength.
- We know we can survive tragedy.

CHAPTER **6**

Listening to Yourself

When we meet real tragedy in life, we can react in two ways—either by losing hope and falling into self-destructive habits, or by using the challenge to find our inner strength. Thanks to the teachings of Buddha, I have been able to take this second way.

—Dalai Lama

After a traumatic event, your entire being gives you all kinds of messages in the forms of feelings, muscle tension, and even, at times, an inability to function. Somewhere deep inside, you are saying: "Help, I'm in trouble! Listen to me. Hear my pain and distress."

How do we answer? Where is peace?

It may seem like you are drowning in an ocean of feelings. To look at the whole is an overwhelming task when you think of all the symptoms of tragedy and grief you checked off on the previous lists. When this happens, we tend to shy away from overpowering emotions.

Your Brain

Our thinking creates our feelings.

If left to its own power, our brain can leap from one place to another in rapid succession. Our brain can be like an untamed wild horse—galloping here and there, kicking up its heels, and going off in every direction at once. It can focus on the past or the future. If left to its own devices, it can sink us into a deep depression or a heightened state of anxiety. Dr. Elizabeth Hoge, from Harvard Medical School, and her fellow researchers found that meditation or mindfulness to reduce stress could lessen anxiety in those who worried excessively, had difficulty sleeping, and were generally irritable.

Journal this for yourself. Just be aware of your mental processes. As you begin to notice how your brain works, your awareness changes the way your brain reacts.

But how do we get past the brain's shotgun approach to reality? Let's begin by focusing on your experience of this moment. Create a mindful moment for yourself.

Mindfulness

Mindfulness is paying attention to *right now*. It's being present with your immediate experience—internally as well as externally. Be aware of this moment's awareness.

I like to think of it as listening to yourself at this place in time. Sit with your immediate experience. Listen externally. Recognize the sound of the air-conditioner or traffic on the road outside. Right now, you are reading this book. Look at the letters on the page. Check out the shapes of the letters and the lines of words. See the white space between paragraphs. Notice your hands holding the book and the flexibility of the book's spine. (Or be aware of your electronic device.) Be aware of your body—where you are sitting. Notice your feet, the feeling in your abdomen, and the sensations in other body parts. Be still and attend to every part of your awareness. Experience the moment and be curious about every aspect of it.

Let's look at your internal experience as well as your external experience—the fear you may feel when you think about a rush of feelings. After you've lived through trauma, the flood of emotions you experience can be overpowering, making you afraid to look at them.

You may say, "I don't want to look at my feelings. I'm scared they will overwhelm me. What if I drown in them? If I connect with my emotions, I'll go so far into them I'm afraid I'll never get out."

Be aware of the fear right now. Notice it guarding you from your feelings. What does it look like? Can you give it a color? A shape? What music would you associate with it? Fear has been defined as an acronym: FEAR (false expectations appearing real). Could that be the case with you?

Sit with the fear. Feel it. Fear has been your friend. It has cautioned you—helped you be watchful, kept you aware of what was going on around you. It was a way for you to keep yourself under control.

Now give it a color.

Give it a shape.

Stand it on its head.

Waggle it in the air.

Make it giggle.

Tell it thanks for helping you.

Make a mental note to watch for it and say hi now that the two of you are friends.

Notice fear whenever it is present and be aware of its contribution to your mental state.

Your Breathing

Check your breathing right now. Is it shallow? Is it faster than normal because of your fear or anxiety?

Just notice your breathing. Be aware of the air coming into your nostrils. Now, notice it filling your lungs, your belly. Watch your abdomen go in and out.

Your breathing can decrease your heart rate and lower your blood pressure. If you slow your breathing and take deeper breaths, you will get more oxygen into your bloodstream so that your thinking will be clearer.

Following are several breathing exercises that may help avert a fearful panic attack and slow your heart rate. All these techniques can be done taking air into your lungs like you usually do, or you can breathe from your diaphragm to expand your air intake. To check your diaphragm breathing, put one hand on your chest. As you breathe in, your chest should remain still. Put your other hand on your diaphragm; it should expand as you breathe in.

1. Four–four–eight
   a. Breathe in slowly through your nose to the count of four.
   b. Hold that breath to the count of four.
   c. Breathe out slowly to the count of eight.
2. Resistance breathing
   a. Breathe in slowly through your nose to the count of four.
   b. Hold your breath to the count of four.
   c. Breathe out slowly through your mouth to the count of eight, pursing your lips.
   d. You can vary these numbers to five or six if you wish, according to how you feel.
3. Equal breathing
   a. Breathe in slowly through your nose to the count of four.
   b. Breathe out slowly through your nose to the count of four.
4. Nostril breathing
   a. With your right thumb, hold your right nostril closed. Breathe in slowly to the count of four through your left nostril.
   b. With your right ring finger, hold your left nostril closed. Breathe out slowly to the count of four through your right nostril.

Using these mindfulness and breathing techniques can help you calm your mind down enough to see your emotions clearly. We've talked about how the brain is affected by trauma, distorting our memories and, sometimes, pushing our reactions out of proportion. It's like taking a step back to view ourselves from outside our body. By viewing what's going on in our brain from a distance, we can begin to modify ourselves. The clarity that comes from this insight brings us one step closer to resolving our issues and finding peace.

Connie's grandmother, age ninety-nine, lived with her. Grandmother got around pretty well with her walker, but Connie put her in the wheelchair much of the time—especially when Grandmother was tired and not too steady on her feet.

Grandmother, Connie, and Connie's young daughter, Mary, had just finished lunch. Grandmother got up from the table and moved herself toward her walker.

"I'm headed for a nap," Grandmother said.

"I'll just wipe Mary's face and be along to help you," Connie said.

Just as Connie finished wiping up Mary's lunch, she heard a thud. She rushed down the hall to see Grandmother slumped against the doorframe—tipped backward. Grandmother had hit her head on the edge of the doorframe. She was still upright, holding on to her walker.

"Help me to bed," Grandmother managed to say.

Connie steadied her and got her onto the bed.

After hitting her head, Grandmother went downhill rapidly. She didn't get out of bed again. She wouldn't eat and took only a little liquid that Connie dripped into her mouth. In two days, Grandmother was dead.

Connie wept as she told this story in my office. "I feel so guilty," she said, shaking and breathing shallowly. "She would still be alive if I had just been there to catch her."

"Just sit with the moment," I told her. "Here is a mindfulness exercise that will lessen your shaking and regulate your breathing."

I suggested, "Be aware of your surroundings. Notice your feet, your legs, your abdomen, and the rest of your body. Focus on your breathing. Take air in slowly to the count of four. Now exhale to the count of four. Notice your nostrils as you breathe. Be aware of your lungs, your abdomen—the life-giving quality of the air."

The shaking stopped. I asked her to sit with her guilt.

"I can't," she said. "It's too overwhelming."

"Continue your breathing, and let's look at it together."

Connie sat back and the tears dripped down her face.

"Close your eyes and tell me: What does your guilt look like? Does it have a color? A shape?"

"It's a dirty white color," Connie said. "It doesn't have a shape. It fills the whole space—kind of like fog."

"What else can you tell me about it?"

"There are memories in the fog. My grandmother reading to me as a child. Us canning peaches." She smiled. "The floor is all sticky. She was a messy cook. Her teaching me to sew a yellow dress with butterflies on it." She began to cry in earnest again. "She was always there for me, and I wasn't there for her."

"You're right in this instance. You weren't there to protect her from falling," I said. "But let's think of the ways you were there for her."

Connie took another deep breath. "I brought her to live with me. I fed her and helped her dress. I brushed her teeth and . . ." Connie recounted other things she had done for Grandmother.

"You weren't perfect, but you were good to her," I said.

"Yes," she said.

"You can keep the dirty white fog of guilt around you if you wish," I said, "but it's holding back your memories from being clear and bright."

"I can see that," she said. "I want my memories to be strong."

Connie and I worked together for a few more sessions. She practiced breathing slowly when she felt overwhelmed. She used her mindfulness, along with other techniques we will learn, to release her guilt and give her memories the clarity she was looking for.

Feelings can seem overwhelming if condensed into a whole package. The urge to discount them or run away can be real. Use your mindfulness skills and other techniques we'll discuss to listen to your feelings, one at a time, in the moment as they present themselves—not in an overpowering wave with your mind running off in every direction at once.

Have your own mindful conversation:
- Sit with your surroundings. Describe them.
- Notice your body—each part.
- Look at your feeling in the moment:
  - Color?
  - Shape?
- Be aware of your breathing. Focus on it.
- Acknowledge that you are not perfect, but you are good.
- If another feeling comes, give it a comfortable place to wait for another mindful moment.
- Take a cleansing breath. Move around. How did that feel?
- Write or draw about it.

Summary

Tragedy can bring a flood of overwhelming feelings. Our brains may engulf us in thoughts and emotions. When this happens, step back and be aware of what your brain is doing. Slow it down with mindful moments.

Mindfulness looks at one moment at a time, making overpowering feelings manageable, one emotion at a time. Breathing exercises can bring your experience into focus. Be aware of the current minute, externally and internally, and attend to every aspect of your specific experience, including your strengths and weaknesses.

Commitment

- Be aware of your brain and the way it works.
- Use your breathing exercises to de-stress yourself and slow down.
- Practice mindfulness each day.
- Be aware of a feeling moment.
- Is it a moment of strength or weakness?
- Accept both your strengths and your weaknesses.

CHAPTER 7

Healing the Whole Person

We can throw stones,
complain about them,
stumble on them,
climb over them,
. . . or build with them.
—William Arthur Ward,
Fountains of Faith

Our Thinking Creates Our Feelings

Many of the popular self-help books today ask readers to step back, assess, and alter their thinking patterns with a mindfulness stance to change their behaviors. It is exciting to see a client stop and look at their behaviors. For, if they do that, they have begun to change their thinking and, therefore, their behaviors. It gives a person a sense of power to realize that they can be in control of their actions by changing their thinking.

Some psychologists suggest that we are separate from our brains. They ask us to evaluate our brains, where the thoughts originate, and change our responses to the world. The premise of these books—that thinking creates feeling—is a popular technique with research to prove those who use this method will have a better quality of life.

Mindfulness (discussed in the preceding chapter) will improve our lives and help us live a more peaceful existence. However, if we have suffered any kind of tragedy, not only do we need to alter our thinking patterns but we must also heal physically and emotionally. Tragedy affects our entire self—physically, mentally, and emotionally. Our entire being needs to heal.

This book addresses the entire spectrum of self-help. It also goes a step beyond the popular self-*help* books of today and becomes a complete self-*healing* book—a way for those of us who have suffered trauma, tragedy, or significant loss to find peace and goodness in a world full of chaos and disaster.

Because of the trauma we have experienced, many of us find ourselves in an uncontrolled state where mental, physical, and emotional memories intrusively bombard us. The goal of healing is to come to a more ordered place where we can rebuild ourselves from the tragedies of the past.

Guided imagery is a time-honored method of meditation and healing. I have found it to be client-friendly because each person chooses their own visualizations according to need.

The creative visualization practice helped many of my clients in their recovery from tragedy. As we have already noted, tragedy stimulates brain centers, causing some to over-function and others to shut down. Anxiety, fear, and depression can overwhelm our physical bodies and our brains. When this happens, it's important to give our mind and body a chance to regroup and heal. Allowing peace and tranquility to be part of our life through creative visualization can help restore us both mentally and physically. According to *ScienceDaily*, imagery can reduce fear and anxiety before surgery, manage stress, and may aid in reducing headaches.

But we must go beyond just imagery to encompass physical, mental, and emotional healing. This process of creating imagery that includes all our senses must be our own. No one else can do this for us. If we are to heal from it, we must use personal internal wisdom in order to mentor ourselves.

It's important not to impose this creative imagination on anyone else. As a therapist, I found the greatest healing took place when the client came up with the visualization ideas, according to the individual issues they were dealing with. Each of us has the power to heal ourselves.

Creative Visualizations

I, unwittingly, began a process like this when I was a child. After my father was killed and I understood that he really wasn't coming back, I visualized the good times we had together. I pictured him reading me stories and rubbing my back. I felt his arms around me every night as I went to sleep.

First, we all need to visually create our own place of safety. Some of the most powerful scenes come from one's childhood. Include all the senses as you envision this place, not just the imagery.

As a child, Rae Jean lived in a chaotic home—her father was often drunk, and her parents spent much of the time fighting. But every summer she spent several weeks with her aunt, who had a cabin in the woods near a lake. In therapy, she created a visualization of this summer experience, including the whispering of the wind in the pines, the coolness of the breeze off the water, the warmth of the summer sun, the sand beneath her toes, the smell of marshmallows roasting over a fire and their delicious taste. Her aunt was always in the background to talk to. Rae Jean could tell her aunt anything, and through their discussions, Rae Jean made healthy decisions as she grew into her teen years. This was a perfect, safe place for her. This imagery was especially healing for her because she was able to meet some of the childhood safety needs missing from life with her parents.

Notice that Rae Jean included sight, sound, touch, smell, feeling, taste, and connection in her meditation. Enjoying time with this visualization daily gave her internal strength and positive connection to the healthy part of herself and her family. This link with self is so important. We all have the tools for healing inside us. But many of us are so disconnected from the internal wisdom we possess, we aren't able to meet our own needs. The negative messages from others and ourselves separate us from the inherent wisdom we all possess, messages like these:

- "You'll never amount to anything."
- "You don't know what you're talking about."
- "You're so stupid."
- "That was a dumb idea."

You get the point.

Rae Jean healed on many levels using this creative visualization. She was able to find the support she needed from her aunt in those visualizations to discount the negative thoughts. We don't need to delve into all of the specifics for Rae Jean. The importance of the meditation came from the fact that the healing had taken place. She used this first mental movie as a jumping-off point to create more of these summer vacation scenes so she could trade them off when she meditated, as she wished.

You can see that if I, as the therapist, had given her a written script, or if she had used one that she found in a meditation book, it wouldn't have been nearly as healing or nearly as effective as the one she created from the depths of her soul.

I also found that when Rae Jean kept a written record of these scenes (a journal), it helped increase the sensory involvement, developed the image to a greater extent, and cemented the movie more clearly in her mind. This also pulls the physical, mental, and emotional healing to a cognitive level so that the brain integrates it as a whole.

For a person who is a survivor of child abuse, a childhood scene probably isn't a good idea. But you can certainly find a time in your life that was safe and use that to visualize your safe place.

Create a Healing Image

To create your own health-giving images, find a safe place in your mind, either real or imagined. Then, develop that image so that it has the healing properties especially for you.

Think outside the box and find something that works for your best good. I had an abuse survivor who created her imagery on the moon, because that was the only place she felt safe at that moment. Another client made a healing hospital on a cloud. It became highly developed as her therapy progressed, with treatment rooms for different abusive issues she suffered.

When you are creating this safe place, it's important that you find a location that is tailored just to you. As you invent your own visual, you are beginning the reconnection with yourself. The abuse survivors that I worked with had a hard time finding a place best for them. One created a beautiful castle under the sea. Another a bunker in the Sahara Desert. You could create a playroom for your inner child. Or build a hospital to heal your body as well as your soul (see chapter 9).

A childhood memory may guide you to select your place. Remember Rae Jean, who spent her summers in a small cabin by a lake? She loved the security she felt there, so that became her safe place.

Think back to pleasurable moments in your childhood. Find a time where you were happy, with no stress or undesirable thinking. If nothing stands out to you from your youth, select a scene from a memorable vacation. Maybe you've even watched a travel show with a place you'd love to visit. Use that if you wish. Don't put any boundaries on yourself in this process. Create something that will bring peace and light to you.

I have several that I like to use. I love walking along the ocean, feeling the sand beneath my bare feet, smelling the salty air, and listening to the waves lap the shore. I also enjoy tramping in the forest with the pines sharing their secrets as they wave their top branches in the wind. It's a peaceful forest message that I love. I always add in the birds and squirrels discussing life. Squirrels especially keep the conversation lively. They can have great debates with the scrub jays. My dad and I meet there often in my visualizations because he loved the forest, and so do I.

Include Sensory Aspects to the Image or Your Experience

You can enhance this image as time goes along. Listen inside, and you will know your innermost needs. The more senses you include in this visual, the more powerful it will be. As you practice your visualizations, the imagery can become more complex and more complete as you incorporate elements such as these:

- Light.
- Dark with stars.
- Touch.
- Taste.
- Sound.
- Smell.
- Connection with others.
- Being alone.

You are welcome to use outside music if you wish. You may also use inner music created in your head, if that works better for you. I've never made a study of what others do, but music plays in my head all the time. If this helps you set the tone of your imagery, use music!

Rae Jean also included an internal porch swing where she and her aunt could cuddle close and watch the stars in the evening. As she developed this imagery, she could feel her body relax. Her muscles moved more freely, and the frequency of her headaches diminished significantly. Her body had stored the tension she felt as a child when she would hide in her room while her drunken father beat her mother.

When you use physical interventions, always keep the memories positive. Be sure they are healing in nature. When you have designed your own visualization, you are ready to use it daily. Find a relaxing place where you won't be disturbed. Surround yourself with tranquility as you wish—a soft couch, soothing music, candles, soft colors, relaxing scents, and the like.

Bring In Support

Surround your safe place with other areas and people to help with this healing. We will talk more about these other areas in later sections of the book. I mention some here to give a sense of what can be done.

Create a wise mentor inside. (See the following chapter.) This guide will be available to you whenever you choose. Sit down with this counselor and talk about your situation—what's happening in your life at the moment and how to handle things. Explore relationships and decide what will be best for you. Think through upcoming events and what your course of action should be. Listen to the words of wisdom given to you.

The wise-mentor experience can be a discussion. But you can also create a feeling mentor that will guide you to experience tastes that you love—a fresh bowl of raspberries, peaches, or whatever you enjoy. Maybe give you a good back rub. This mentor could hold you while you grieve your loss like the image of my father when I was a child. Find ways to experience sights and smells and sounds with this guide.

Outside Thoughts

If other thoughts float in to disturb your visual, glide them off into the sunlight. You can visit these ideas later if necessary. See if there is a pattern to the extraneous thoughts. Make a mental note to explore them another time if you think it necessary.

If this is a healing visual, use it as long as it's needed and then create another one—move on to the next phase of creating a healthier you.

Starting Your Creative Visualization

If you already have a meditation practice, please continue it. Here is a system that has worked well for me and many of my clients:

1. Enjoy the mindfulness of this moment. Be aware of your external environment. Notice your feet, your ankles, and mentally move upward on your body. Find gratitude inside you for who you are.
2. Begin access to your internal state by becoming aware of your breathing. Notice the air you take in. Be attentive to its life-giving properties. Breathe deeply. Let the air fill your lungs down into your belly. Release it. Set the rhythm to a thoughtful pace—one that works for you.
3. Some clients enter their centering place by climbing ten steps—counting them slowly—along with their breathing. One . . . Two . . . Three . . . Four . . . Others prefer to descend the steps.
4. Walk into your safe place. Enjoy the sights, sounds, smells, tastes, and connection with self. Be curious about your place. Learn all you can of its details and be open to new discoveries—things you hadn't been aware of before.

Check in with your breathing during this process. Be aware of your body through this procedure. Feel your feet, ankles, legs, torso, arms, shoulders, neck, and head. Notice any tension in them and float it away into the light.

If you find distracting thoughts entering your daily practice, be aware of them. Acknowledge them, save them on an internal bulletin board to think about later, or float them away into the light.

5. When you have finished your meditation, thank those inside who have helped you, and give thanks for your safe internal setting. Then, descend the stairs and slowly become aware of your external surroundings.
6. I always like to spend a minute in gratitude for who I am and what I'm about. Then, go forward and have a great day.

This mind and body centering will take some practice. Since our brain can take us to any and every direction at once, it's helpful to center yourself through this meditation process. Connect with your internal wisdom and find the peace and light you seek.

It's important to be able to go into your feelings and grieve your losses, but you also have to get up out of them and do daily life. Meditation will teach you the art of accessing your feelings, but it will also give you the skills to get up out of them and continue living during this period of your life.

If I'm feeling especially tense or down, sometimes I do an extra creative visualization on the fly—when I'm waiting for my grandkids after school or when I'm sitting in the doctor's office. This is okay, but when you are in the process of recovering from a significant trauma in your life, take more time, as outlined earlier. Use this "fly" time as an extra. Don't let it replace your daily meditation.

To keep myself centered, I meditate daily with my creative visualizations. It brings peace and joy to my life.

Summary

Creative visualization, along with mindfulness, will aid the healing process to help you reconnect with yourself. Create a pleasant image from childhood or any other place that is soothing. This image can be real place or an imagined one. Surround yourself with the support you need. This type of visualization is more effective if all the senses are included—touch, taste, sight, sound, and smell. Add internal or external music if you wish. Tailor this visualization to fit your healing needs. After you develop it, write about it to further enhance the images and cement them in your mind.

Make creative visualizations a part of your routine. Find joy and be blessed in this pursuit.

Commitment

- Invent a creative visualization that will be healing for you.
- Add all the senses to your mental movie.
- Journal a description of it.
- Meditate with it daily to feel its peace and light.
- Set a time and place to meditate daily.
- Make your internal safe place.
- Add to it as you wish.

CHAPTER 8

Creative Visualizations—An Internal Guide

Adversity introduces a man to himself.
—Author Unknown

We all have wisdom inside us to help us heal if we will just look for it. We must access it in order to reach our full potential. This process of connecting with yourself will give you an internal strength to center your life and face the trials that come your way.

Use your creative visualization process during your meditation time to access this internal guide.

1. Practice mindfulness.
2. Slow and count your breathing.
3. Climb the stairs to the count of ten.
4. Step into your creative visualization.

5. Look for an internal guide.
6. Return from your meditation by the stairs.
7. Give thanks for your safe internal setting.
8. Give gratitude for your existence.

While you are in your safe place, look around for your internal guide. Where will he or she be? In your safe place or in another area? Take your time to discover what's there. What kind of surroundings do you find? Describe this mentor:

- What are they wearing?
- Describe their personality.
- Is this someone you know?
- If so, greet them warmly and reminisce over old times.
- If not, get to know them. Find out their likes and dislikes.
- What is their background?
- How do you know they will be of help?

Your internal guide, or counselor, might be someone you know— an older version of yourself, a person in your life right now, a family member or friend that has passed on, or even a wise celebrity. One of my clients found the Dalai Lama when she looked internally. Someone else I worked with had an internal board meeting with several people to discuss things. Another client used me for her internal guide.

Maybe your insight doesn't come from a person. One abuse survivor I counseled had a tree for her source of understanding. Another accessed her spring of knowledge from deep in the earth.

Put no preconceived ideas on yourself. Listen internally and follow your own insight. Think outside the box, and you will discover your own wisdom.

Describe your internal guide:

_____

_____

_____

_____

Take some time to get acquainted with your internal guide. You need to develop a relationship with this entity. Don't rush yourself. Get to know this counselor, or mentor, and build a relationship. Question them about their ideas and beliefs. Don't accept blindly what they say. The two of you need to make your decisions together.

Recognize that the wisdom of your guide comes from you. There will be lots of messages that your mind will provide, which you get to sort through as you dialogue with your guide and mentor. This is an opportunity to figure out which thoughts and options are truest for you.

My internal guide has always been my father. He is great to talk with. He listens and tells me what he thinks. But he has always encouraged me to make my own decisions. There was a time in my life I wasn't listening to him. As I grew out of my childhood, I let go of my relationship with him somewhat.

During my young adult years, I made some decisions without discussing things with him, and I have doubted the wisdom of some of the paths I have taken. There have been times when, in the midst of a trial, I have questioned my judgment, feeling like I have been taken for a fool and made a totally bad decision. But as life has gone along, I have reengaged with my wise mentor-father, and he has helped me see that even my "bad" decisions have added to my wisdom and helped me become a better person.

Some of you might say, "I've never had good judgment; I know I don't have any wisdom inside me." You may be afraid to access the insight you have inside.

Here are some reasons you might hesitate to access this internal guide:

- I'm too busy to stop and think what's best.
- I don't have confidence in my decisions.
- I've made too many bad decisions already. I don't trust myself.
- I don't know how to listen to myself.
- My thoughts are racing. I can't pick out which idea is best.
- I make a decision, but I always change my mind.
- Someone else has always made my choices for me.
- I don't like to plan ahead. I enjoy making spontaneous decisions.

The list can go on and on. It will be as varied as the number of people we ask.

If choosing a guide seems like a difficult task for you, use a wise teacher and study their writings. Come to know this person well—the things they stand for. Then, as you engage them for an internal guide, you'll know how they would advise you because you are aware of their wisdom. The client who used me for an internal guide didn't have enough confidence in herself to make decisions, so she made me her guide. She was really setting her own course in life herself, but until her connection with herself and her confidence in herself was better, she used an image of me to help her sort through all her thoughts.

If you want to become your best self, practice listening internally. Generate this internal guide so you can work through the tragedy you've experienced and become the person you've always wanted to be.

In my book *Becoming Free* I outline a method for decision-making that includes the following steps:

- Brainstorm all possible solutions.
- Consider each idea separately.
- Study the pros and cons of each.
- Choose the best idea for you.

Use this outline internally with your mentor to decide how you will proceed.

After you've talked to your guide and mentor, I recommend journaling about what you've discovered and decided. It will cement the development of your experience more fully in your mind and lead you to a greater understanding of yourself.

Look inside to find your internal guide. Work together to make your life the best it can be. This guide can also be a friend and companion. Sometimes, you may want to just hang out together, even if you don't have any conflict to resolve. Maybe you'll even sit in the sun or smell the flowers.

Know that life is good.

Summary

Choosing a wise mentor is a wonderful way to connect (or reconnect) with yourself. Follow your steps to mindfulness meditation. When you are in your safe place, look around for a guide and companion. This person might be someone you know or a wise teacher. Talk with each other and get acquainted. Study him or her so that you can give a detailed description in your journal. Talk about the decision-making process together. After your meditation, journal about the experience to help you remember and cement it in your mind. Congratulations! You are beginning to connect with yourself.

Commitment

- Think about creating an internal guide.
- During your creative visualization, find this mentor.
- Get acquainted.
- Discuss how you will work together.

CHAPTER 9

Creative Visualizations—An Internal Hospital

Grown-ups never understand anything by themselves, and it is tiresome for children to be always and forever explaining things to them.

—Antoine de Saint-Exupéry, *The Little Prince*

Think outside the box as you create your internal healing world. I'm not going to share all the ways my clients used creative visualizations to gain strength, but several of them envisioned internal hospitals. This was so powerful, I decided to detail it for you here.

I had a young adult client, Brenda, who grew up with some fears and anxieties. When she became engaged to be married, her anxieties reached the point where she felt the need to seek counseling to help her through some of her worries. Brenda had an extreme fear of needles and shots. When she had her wisdom teeth out, she fainted during the procedure because of the anxiety.

In our first few sessions, I learned that Brenda had been born three months premature. Her birth weight was very low, and she spent the first two months of her life in the neonatal unit of a children's hospital.

As we talked about her beginnings, she brought in a newspaper article about her early birth with a picture of her in the incubator—her tiny body hooked up to all sorts of tubes.

As she looked at her own history, she could see that her fears may have come from the early trauma surrounding her birth and the time she spent in the hospital.

She worried that when she had children, she wouldn't be able to handle them being inoculated. The child inside herself was still frail and frightened.

I explained the concepts behind creative visualization.

1. Practice mindfulness.
2. Slow and count your breathing.
3. Climb the stairs to the count of ten.
4. Step into your creative visualization.
5. Spend time with your internal guide.
6. Return from your meditation by the stairs.
7. Give thanks for your safe internal setting.
8. Give gratitude for your existence.

Brenda wanted to use creative visualization to address her anxieties. She took a little time to decide how she could soothe that tiny premature baby that still intruded into her present life. Brenda chose to create a hospital for the small infant because Brenda felt the baby was too little to thrive elsewhere. But she gave her an angel-mentor who kept her alive without all the needles and IVs and tubes.

Her reasoning was that she could heal herself as a tiny infant—physically as well as emotionally—so that the needles and tubes wouldn't be an issue for her. This would take body work as well as mind work. To start, during her daily meditations, Brenda created the visuals of her hospital. She detailed this healing place as a large open room, not a tiny enclosed incubator like the one she had really been in. Her angel was in the room with her at all times.

Daily, the angel-nurse soothed, cuddled, and caressed this premature infant, paying specific attention to the areas of her body where the monitors and needles had been placed. As Brenda practiced this imagery, she could feel herself gaining internal strength. I suggested that she extend her therapy to include external body work (which is discussed in more detail in the next chapter). She found an experienced massage therapist to visit once a month and began practicing yoga.

I've kept in touch with Brenda over the years. She has had several children. Doctor visits still aren't her favorite thing to do, but she can get through them—and the shots—without fainting.

Here's one more example of a creative visualized hospital: Jane was an abuse survivor. She had many issues, including being battered as a child. Muscle tension caused her to walk with rigidity. Because her arm had been broken and not set correctly, she had limited use of it. Even though her present doctors surgically repaired the arm, Jane still couldn't use it as she wished. She had a great physical therapy team that helped her regain some movement, but she wasn't satisfied with her range of motion.

Her creative visualization included a hospital where a caring doctor saw to young Jane's every need right after the battery episode that had broken her arm. Her internal doctor set the arm, massaged it after it healed, and had her exercise it.

Jane's arm improved with the internal visualizations and the support of the physical therapy team who helped with the external body work. She said she felt it was as important to heal those early body memories as it was to heal as the adult arm. She still doesn't have full use of her elbow, but her muscles are more relaxed and her movement is much improved.

Do you need a hospital to heal a part of you? Maybe you didn't go through a medical trauma. Maybe your body hasn't been significantly injured. But perhaps, like me, you lost a loved one tragically, which broke your heart. Would visualizing a medical team supporting that broken heart help? Is there another part of you that is ailing?

Create a healing program that will mend you internally as well as externally. Set a regimen that will help you become your very best.

You cannot erase the tragedy, but you
can mend yourself enough to be an
example of the power of regeneration.

Summary

Build an internal hospital as part of your creative visualization if you wish. Set the healing therapies according to your deficits or injuries. Internal body work and external body work go hand in hand in the healing process. Use both in combination.

Commitment

- Create an internal hospital as part of your therapy.
- Add internal caregivers that will enhance your healing.
- Meditate daily to allow muscle tension and rigidity to melt into healing.
- Include external body work to enhance the internal healing.

CHAPTER 10

Body Work and Trauma

*Neuroscience research shows that the only way
we can change the way we feel is by becoming
aware of our inner experience and learning to
befriend what is going inside ourselves.*
—Bessel A. van der Kolk

Traumatization is stored not only in our memory and emotions but also
in our bodies. As I worked with clients, I came to understand that if
they wanted to free themselves from past suffering, the release must be
physical, emotional, and mental. I advised them to do some body work
(large-muscle activity) along with their creative visualization. While
research in the area of physical exercise to reduce PTSD symptoms is
in its beginning stages, there is evidence to suggest that body work is
effective as an adjunct treatment.

As you settle on a program that will work for you, please remember
to tailor it to your individual needs. My clients decided on a variety of
physical healing techniques. Following are a couple of examples.

Kelly had been sexually abused by her father from the age of eight
through her teen years. Even though he had passed away, she couldn't

let go of her anger toward him. Her tension-filled body exhibited her rage in all she did. Stiff, angular movements accompanied the critical words that spilled from her mouth. Each time I met with her, I could see tightness enveloping her entire body.

Deep breathing and visualization helped her release some of her tension. She created a safe place and a wise counselor. But when she got upset, nothing could override the rigidity that consumed her small, wiry frame. I tried to get her to do some muscle relaxation exercises during our sessions, but she wasn't responsive to them. She wanted something more focused toward her abuse. We talked about what kind of body work would be best for her.

During each abuse episode with her father, she had pushed and shoved him, unsuccessfully, to fight him off. She assumed that was the reason she felt the muscle tension primarily in her arms and legs.

She decided to take kickboxing lessons because that focused on her extremities. Kelly also thought it seemed like an empowering sport for women. She signed up for lessons at the gym, but she went a step beyond. She found a large punching bag at a secondhand store. She hung it in her garage and drew an outline of her father on the leather just high enough for her to punch and kick it. Every day, as part of her healing regimen, Kelly kickboxed his body, yelling the mantras she had written especially for him. After each hard workout, she could feel the rigidity leave her muscles. She could feel the physical as well as mental release.

At the end of each session, Kelly soaked in a warm bath with scented candles to soothe her body and release the feelings she had experienced. When you do body work like this, also be sure to do some creative visualizations afterward that will bring peace to your system. Infuse yourself with light and love in a way that works for you. Remember, we need to be able to go into our feelings, but we need to be able to get out of them as well.

Kelly came to love working out. As she progressed in her healing process, she let go of the boxing and began taking other classes at the gym. She transitioned from anger—specific to her father—to love of physical exercise. She had done the deep muscle release necessary for her healing, and now Kelly liked the way she felt when she was in good physical shape. She continued to keep her body toned and fit.

This is an extreme example of body healing for an abuse survivor.

If you decide to do something like this, there are several guidelines to follow:

1. Do not inflict physical violence on yourself or other people.
2. Make sure you are physically safe while working out.
3. Make sure others are physically safe.
4. Work alone or with another adult as your coach if you wish.
5. Ensure there are no children present for *any* part of this process.
6. Use this as a healing tool and move beyond it to another form of physical exercise, as Kelly did.

Children store abuse in their bodies as well as adults. Here is the story of a young girl I worked with.

Chloe, an active four-year-old, came to therapy with her mother. Mom had walked in on a twelve-year-old stepson touching Chloe's private parts inappropriately. Mom was angry at the stepson and had her own issues to work through after Chloe's healing.

Chloe could verbalize exactly what happened, and we talked about touching—okay touching and not-okay touching. We discussed how she could keep herself safe.

Art mediums are a good way to help children (and adults) release their trauma. I gave Chloe the choice of drawing with art materials or creating from clay. She chose the clay.

Chloe built an image of her stepbrother and smashed it with her fist. "Leave me alone," she shouted to the clay over and over. She repeated this process of building, smashing, and yelling for the entire hour-long session.

That night her mother reported that Chloe was tired, wanting to be cuddled and rocked for the evening. Chloe had gone into her feelings and then needed some soothing time afterward to get out of them.

For the next several therapy sessions, Chloe continued to emote through different art mediums, but never with the intensity she had done that first session. After several visits, she had let go of the incident. Mom and her new husband had made protective arrangements so Chloe knew she was safe. Incident closed for Chloe.

Many of my clients used workouts at the gym, dance, kickboxing, and other conventional methods as part of their healing program, along with their creative visualizations and their mantras. The type of workouts you choose will be entirely up to you. I don't know that there are any specific types of workouts that fit with certain types of trauma. The choice will be yours as to the exercise interests you have and the places in your body that need to release built-up tension. Yoga is also an excellent full-body restoration program. Other techniques a survivor might explore are Watsu, holistic health practices, chiropractic, and acupuncture.

Massage therapy is another method that can aid the healing process. (There are even no-touch therapies that can be helpful.) Check out shiatsu techniques, Reiki, and Swedish massage, among other massage practices. If you decide on any of these methods, be sure you find a reputable therapist—one who has had experience with trauma survivors and is knowledgeable about the craft.

It is up to you to determine if you need to share any of your history with a trainer or therapist. Certainly, if you think that a particular practice in a self-defense class will trigger your trauma and perhaps endanger you or your sparring partner, it could be wise to mention it. But no trainer or massage therapist should be used in place of a professional counselor. Discuss with your therapist or your internal guide just how much, if at all, you should share as you start body work.

Find a program that works best for you. If you already have an interest or an expertise in any physical, full-body healing practice, be sure to continue to incorporate it into your life.

There are a couple of specific programs that I will briefly mention that can be part of your healing regimen if you are interested. Tension and Trauma Release Exercises (TRE®), developed by David Berceli, PhD, in his work with trauma survivors in Africa and the Middle East seem to be effective and are beginning to be researched.

This technique claims that vibrating and shaking the entire body helps discharge tension in the muscles. If it is done in a secure setting, this practice will aid the body in returning to a natural state of equilibrium. I have not used this method and have had no experience with it. Check it out at this website if you wish: https://traumaprevention .com/what-is-tre/.

Another promising body-centered treatment model, Somatic Experiencing®, has been successful in working with PTSD survivors. Since trauma alters the natural body cycles, this technique helps survivors regain their natural rhythm again. You can learn more at this website: http://www.socialworktoday.com/archive/090915p12.shtml.

As you can see, there are many ways to unleash the tension stored in the body after experiencing a tragedy. Do your own research and find a method of release that works for you while following these guidelines:

- Remember to keep yourself and others safe.
- Remember that when you go into your feelings, you need a plan to get out of them as well.

Healing doesn't mean that the tragedy never existed, it means that tragedy no longer controls your being.

Begin with a therapist if you don't know where to start with your body work. You can also brainstorm with your internal guide in your creative imagery. Discuss with your internal guide or your outside therapist the options: Would it be most healing to find body work that was relaxing or empowering? Do you want to take a class or have individual sessions?

This work isn't a one-time activity. It needs to be an ongoing process. As you continue to follow your program, the trauma you experienced will no longer control your life. You will be free to enjoy the gifts you received from this exercise.

Summary

Body work will release the stored muscle tension that occurred during trauma. A healing program that includes a physical release will give you a greater quality of life. If you are involved in an exercise program, continue it. If you haven't started one yet, decide with your internal guide what would be best for you. Study each method and begin your workouts.

Commitment

- Study the workout programs that interest you.
- Choose the best one for you.
- Begin your workouts.
- Continue your exercise program until your muscles have released their memory of the trauma.
- Set a regular workout program after your healing. Keep your body in good shape.

CHAPTER **11**

Putting It All Together—Physical, Mental, and Emotional Recovery

Tragedy is a tool for the living to gain wisdom, not a guide by which to live.
—Robert F. Kennedy,
"Conflict in Vietnam and at Home"

A tragedy or traumatic experience is logged in our body in several ways. We not only have a memory of the incident in our brain, but we carry it with us emotionally and physically as well. As we begin to heal ourselves, we must consider a comprehensive treatment program to be able to walk beyond what has happened to us.

Bill made an appointment and came into my office to discuss a recent trauma he had experienced. He sat forward in his chair—back straight, neck straining, and leg muscles twitching.

Bill started by explaining that he and his friend Adam loved to ice-fish on a lake in northern Minnesota. Every December, they enjoyed an annual fishing trip. On one cold, frosty morning, they hit their limit within several hours. They decided to drive their snowmobiles around before returning to shore.

Adam urged Bill to follow him, running his snowmobile from the safe harbor of the bay out onto the shelf ice of the lake. No one knew how thick or thin the ice was. But everyone, including Adam, understood the shelf ice could give way at any time.

Bill crossed and uncrossed his legs in my office when he mentioned that while he worried about following Adam, he was afraid to tell his friend no. After all, Bill reasoned, they'd done this before, and it was December and the shelf ought to be thick enough to hold them.

At first, they ran close to the shore, but then Adam edged his way out onto the open ice, farther from land. Bill felt nervous, but he followed about a quarter mile behind.

Bill's fists were clenched when he recalled seeing the ice under Adam crack and break. He remembered Adam's shout piercing the morning air. "Help! I'm going down!" Adam and his machine sank.

Bill pulled a little closer, but there was a crack in the ice near him as well. He left his machine to idle, but he couldn't drive any closer. He climbed off and raced toward his friend. The ice gave way before Bill reached the place Adam went down.

Bill plunged into the lake and gasped with shock in the cold water.

Adam's head came to the surface.

Bill could see the frantic look in Adam's eyes. Bill lunged for his friend but couldn't reach him.

Adam went down and was lost. Bill couldn't see him under the water. Icy wetness weighed Bill's winter clothes. He could feel himself sinking—the cold was numbing him. What if he couldn't get to the surface? He frantically paddled back to the ice ledge and pulled himself up onto the shelf. He lay there exhausted.

With the cracks in the ice, he was afraid to stand for fear his body weight would break the ice further. He inched back to his snowmobile on his belly. Shaking and partially paralyzed from cold, he crawled onto the machine, managed to put it in gear, and turned back to the shore.

Bill slumped in his chair and had his head in his hands at this point.

He still couldn't believe it. His friend of twenty years was gone. He felt sick to his stomach—like he was going to throw up.

After giving Bill another moment to recover, I asked him what he did and felt. He was dazed. Frozen. His gloves stuck to the handle bars. When he reached the shore, he ripped his hand loose and stopped the machine. He yelled for help.

Others were close at hand and called 911. But it was too late—Adam was gone.

Bill sat up straight again, opening and closing his fists. "One minute, Adam was there, and the next, he was gone." Bill put his head down again, his legs twitching with intensity. "I still feel sick when I think about it. I should have told him I wouldn't go out onto the shelf." He twisted his fingers.

"I came to Vegas to get out of Minnesota, thinking I would be able to forget. But I just can't let it go. It's my fault he's dead."

Bill's reaction wasn't just emotional. I could see the distress in Bill's behaviors in my office. He obviously still held on to the tragedy that happened six months earlier, even though he moved halfway across the country. Many times, people think a geographic transition will help a situation. It almost never does. We take ourselves with us wherever we go.

Bill continues reliving the trauma, keeping himself stuck. He has overwhelming guilt because he couldn't save Adam. He's not only re-experiencing the mental image of the trauma, but the tension he felt in his frozen hands is still there. He's mentally visualizing the accident, emotionally feeling sadness and guilt, and physically remembering his hands stuck to the snowmobile.

As we talked, I explained that our thinking creates our feelings, but that with tragedy, the response goes much deeper than just the thinking process. His memory of the tragedy also included his emotional and physical state.

Considering this, Bill leaned forward in his chair and clenched and unclenched his jaw. I asked him to be mindful of this moment—to sit back and be aware of his body and his breathing. As he focused on his breathing, his hands rested on the arms of his chair. As his body began to relax, I asked him to just sit with the trauma of the moment when Adam went down.

Could he note his strength in that memory?

Bill began to breathe faster.

We took a minute for him to slow his breathing down with his counting.

"Now, back to the memory," I said. "Can you see the good things that you did?"

"Yes," he said. "I tried to save my friend."

"Name the things you did," I said.

"I drove out as close to Adam as I could. Then, I walked out on the ice until I fell into the water myself. I still tried to reach him, but I couldn't." His voice cracked with emotion.

Again, Bill's legs tensed, and he balled his hands into fists.

"Slow your breathing and relax your hands," I said. "Be aware of the moment. You are here in the office, recounting the memory. It took a lot of courage to do what you did."

"I guess."

"What about your weakness in the memory?"

Bill put his head in his hands again. "I should have told him not to go out onto the ice shelf. I shouldn't have followed him."

"You're wishing you could change your actions," I said.

"Yes, yes." His head came up, and there were tears in his eyes.

"Be aware of your full memory—some good feelings and some regrets," I said. "Breathe in. Breathe out."

Bill focused on his breathing again. His hands and leg muscles relaxed.

In this exercise, Bill looked at his reaction to the incident and could see the positive as well as the negative. Changing from an uncontrolled process to a controlled pattern of being aware of his thoughts gave him a greater understanding of his experience.

I explained the process of creative visualization:

1. Practice mindfulness.
2. Slow and count your breathing.
3. Climb the stairs to the count of ten.
4. Step into your creative visualization.
5. Be aware of your breathing through your visualization process. Keep yourself grounded.
6. Return from your meditation by the stairs.
7. Give thanks for your safe internal setting.
8. Give gratitude for your existence.

I told Bill he could write his own script. When Bill began thinking about his visualization, he wanted to write it so that he saved Adam from drowning. I gently explained that he couldn't bring Adam back to life—as much as he desperately wanted to. He broke down in tears. (When we lose a loved one, I wonder if the grieving process is ever completely over. I know that, at least in my case, it's not.)

Instead of trying to change what had happened, Bill decided that he would focus on a positive time he spent with Adam. He chose a summer fishing trip where they had saved a young boy from drowning. He said it felt good to remember the two of them saving a life.

While he was focusing on this image, I gave him a stress ball for each hand. I had him concentrate on his strong and capable hands, providing life-giving assistance. He gave his attention to their movement: lifting the young boy out of the water (he squeezed the balls), helping him onto the bench in the boat (he gripped the balls), pressing on his chest during CPR (he pressed the balls). Bill reported that after that, he could feel his hands relax each time he used this visualization. "That was a good day," he said.

Bill had other body work to do in the sessions that followed—releasing the sick feeling in his stomach and the tension in the rest of his body from being in the water and crawling across the ice.

Before he left therapy, he scripted other scenes, one of which put Adam in heaven with his daughter, who had died a few years earlier. They relaxed in a beautiful heavenly park, sitting on a bench swing, laughing and talking.

With this work, Bill could begin to let go of his guilt and anxiety over Adam's death and feel happy for his friend. Bill finished his sessions with me with renewed strength to share his story with others in an effort to help survivors involved with drowning victims. "If I can get through this, others can, too. I feel so relieved to move on with my life."

Many times, people think a few therapy sessions will "fix" the problem and that they can forget it and go on with life. But a tragedy like this doesn't go away that easily. It won't control Bill's life anymore, but he will always remember. The gift in this is that he will be able to help others who find themselves in traumatic situations to see that there is life after the trials.

Healing is a process, not an event.

Summary

Creative visualizations in combination with body work can help us move beyond the mental, emotional, and physical trauma of an incident. The visualization steps include:

1. Practice mindfulness.
2. Slow and count your breathing.
3. Climb the stairs to the count of ten.
4. Step into your creative visualization.
5. Be aware of your breathing through your visualization process. Keep yourself grounded.
6. Return from your meditation by the stairs.
7. Give thanks for your safe internal setting.
8. Give gratitude for your existence.

The ability to remember but let go of the trauma is a gift that can help others seeking healing from their own tragedy.

Commitment

- Spend mindful moments.
- Look at the positive in your behavior.
- Look at the things you wish were different.
- Create your own visualization.
- Include the body work associated with it.

PART 3

Grief and the Healing Process

An Afghanistan Wounded Warrior
Amelia

June 2011: we had just come home from a family wedding. Ben, our son, had been with us from Afghanistan on military leave. He had just gotten back to the Middle East when the phone rang. It was July 1, about 6:00 a.m.

I thought, *This can't be good*, and of course, it wasn't. The call came from Fort Drum, which was where Ben was stationed. They said he had been injured. He had been the one with the metal detector, looking for roadside bombs. The Taliban had made their explosives of plastic and covered them with wood, so the metal detector didn't pick them up. In that first phone call, they told us Ben had lost both his legs.

After that first phone call, I wanted to vomit. I sobbed and cried and felt sick. My extended family and people from the church came over when they heard. That first day, we just sat there at the dining room table. We sat all day. Not talking. Not saying anything.

At church a few Sundays before, I heard a quote about Job. His grief was so great, Job's friends couldn't even talk about it. They just sat with him. It was the same for me that first day. There was nothing anyone could do. We just sat.

I felt ill. I couldn't eat and I couldn't sleep, though my husband made sure I did both. That's the place I was in, and I was going to be there for a long time. There was a rock in the pit of my stomach, and I was helpless. There was no contact with Ben. I couldn't see him or touch him or hold him, and my information about him wasn't complete.

I decided that very first day:
- I will hang on.
- I will choose faith.
- I will choose hope.
- I will not be bitter.

I had recently given a lesson at church about choosing faith. That was a little miracle in my life. I felt very blessed to have given that lesson. Some people think you have faith or you have hope, but you don't get them automatically. They are a choice. And I had to revisit that choice many times during this trial.

After the initial phone call, the Army had someone telephone every twelve hours to give us an update. In further updates, they talked only about Ben losing his left leg. They never said anything about his losing his right leg, so I asked about it.

The girl couldn't tell anything from the report she was reading. The Army must have had a call center that telephoned us. These people weren't medical personnel; these updates were their full-time job. They would just read the report, and they didn't understand what they were reading.

So I had my doctor come over one night, and he read the report. Ben still had his right leg. That was a miracle right there.

Because something so awful had happened, I was grateful to know he had lost one leg and not two. It was a little blessing to help me appreciate that it was only one leg.

I found out later that he was taken to the hospital in Kandahar right after the explosion.

Immediately after we found out, my sister got on the phone with our church to see if there was anyone in Kandahar that could give Ben a blessing. I didn't even know it. There were church people there, and they went to give Ben a blessing. But the hospital personnel wouldn't let them in. The church men kept going back, and finally, the fourth time, they were allowed in to give him a blessing. He had several surgeries in Kandahar. Then he was flown to Germany, where he had several more procedures.

One of the first things the Army asked me was, "Do you have a passport so you can come to Germany?"

Because of all his internal injuries, they planned to fly Ben to Germany and have me meet him there. I found out months later that the only reason they arranged for me to go to Germany was to say goodbye because it looked like Ben could die. But Ben didn't die. Another incredible miracle.

Ben had so many abdominal injuries—he was nearly split in half. The surgeons in Germany closed his wounds so he could travel to the States.

A week after the accident, he was flown to Walter Reed National Military Medical Center in Washington, DC. When he got there, they had to keep opening him up because of infection. The land mine had blasted up into him. During the week at Walter Reed, he almost starved to death because they did so many surgeries on him—almost every other day.

Ben stayed in a hospital for two years. During this time, I continually had to revisit my choice to choose faith and hope. I had to review it again and again and again as I stayed with him for ten months.

It was worse that it happened to Ben rather than to me. When we were in the hospital, I would think, *I wish I could change places with him.* He had to have a skin graft on his right leg. I wanted to give him my skin, but I couldn't because then he would have to take anti-rejection drugs.

When he was struggling emotionally, I wanted to have a mind meld so he would know the things I knew because I have lived longer, but, of course, that couldn't happen. I would have traded places with him in a heartbeat. He is such a great young man. I watched him be cheerful and upbeat and noble in the midst of all the pain and struggle.

I began a blog right after all this happened because so many people loved us and were praying for us. I wanted to keep everyone updated. And while writing was therapeutic and I'm glad the blog is there, I choose not to go back and read it again.

When Ben was first flown to Walter Reed, my husband (Ben's stepfather) and I met him there. The doctor on call visited with us. It was a Saturday night, and there weren't many people around, so the doctor took some time with us. He was an anesthesiologist, and he told us in no uncertain terms about all the surgeries Ben would have to have.

"He'll make it, though, because he's young and strong," the doctor said.

His heart rate the first couple of days never got below 160. If that had happened to one of us, our hearts would have given out.

I remember all those little steps on Ben's journey toward healing. He had horrible hallucinations at first. He would see men at the window trying to shoot him. He got to the point where he could say, "I'm seeing something over there. Is it real?" That was a big milestone.

The doctors gave him a pump to control his own pain meds. The doctors try not to let the patient go up and down on the pain meds, because then they don't associate a wonderful sense of relief with the meds. The pump just keeps them steady. Still, it was difficult for him to get off the drugs.

Nine months into his two-year hospital stay, the hospital staff encouraged him to go on a snowboarding trip to Colorado with friends. Reluctantly, he went. He got back late at night. He thought I was asleep and didn't want to disturb me, but I could hear him. He got into bed and just sobbed and sobbed. It was the only time I heard him really cry. I never knew what he cried about. Maybe it was just the difficulty of what he would have to do for the rest of his life. That night was a rough one for him and for me.

I would not wish this kind of tragedy to happen to anyone, but I am grateful for the beauty that was all around us, even through the sadness. There were many programs set up at Walter Reed by Vietnam vets. When the Vietnam vets came home, they didn't get any support. There were no programs for them. But, because of their own trauma, they are there for the wounded warriors now.

One man takes the wounded guys and their families out to a nice restaurant every Friday night. Another guy sits in the lobby so he can talk to the wounded. He took Ben to see a couple of Washington Nationals games. Another guy made a personalized cane for each of the vets. Those Vietnam vets turned their tragedy into something good. And their support made a huge difference in our lives.

I wanted Ben to do all the Friday night dinners. I wanted him to do them sooner than he was ready. He was angry and upset, and I had to learn to let people feel what they feel. There were some days he couldn't overcome the anger, but those became less and less frequent over time.

One of the best things I learned was to let people into my life. I learned to allow people to help me. I had no choice. I was down so low, I didn't have any pride left. I felt really humble. What a blessing it was to accept that. You allow people to bless you and that blesses them.

When they came in to take Ben for an operation or to do something they didn't want me to see, I went for a walk. You have to take care of the basics. Exercise helped me a lot.

There was a couple—the husband was a Vietnam vet and an amputee—that brought cookies, and the husband would talk to the guys. The first time I met his wife, I began to cry, and she held me in her arms while I wept. She knew that was what I needed. I don't even know how we greeted each other. I'd never been down so low; I didn't think I could get any lower. In what lifetime would I ever be grateful that Ben had lost only one leg and not two? But in those impossible moments, you have an innate capacity to choose faith and hope. You choose that from the beginning. You have to look for the tender mercies. This woman and all the others who offered their time and love were just a few of the tender mercies that supported my family in our crisis.

I didn't think there was anything I could do for anybody else, but looking back there was. All of the families would sit in the hospital waiting room together while our sons or husbands were in surgery. Some people had a wall up, and I couldn't reach them, but others had let their facade down. It was like we had our own little support group. When I held someone and let them cry, I would be so grateful that I had done a little something because everyone had been so good to me.

Ben and I were sitting on the hospital's porch one afternoon when a couple came to sit with us. Their son had been in the hospital for two years, and he had had so many infections that after two years, he still didn't have his prosthetic arm. When I saw them, I had all these dreams that maybe Ben could be friends with their son. But their son had struggled himself. He'd had addictions to pain killers. He had a lot of psychological problems that Ben didn't have. I remember thinking this afternoon visit didn't help me at all.

When they were ready to leave, the dad said, "This has been so good. It's been wonderful to talk to someone who understands." When they left, I wanted to cry because I'd been so selfish, wanting to be helped myself rather than helping someone else.

Small kindnesses were essential. I got to see a receptionist every day. She was always so kind and sweet and cheery to me. She lifted me with her smile and friendly manner.

And there were people we didn't even know who sent packages of cookies and nuts and special treats. There were so many anonymous acts. I was touched with the goodness of the world.

One Saturday, a young girl had gone to an orchard and picked peaches and brought them to the hospital to distribute to everyone. Every day some kindness was being extended to me.

I haven't forgotten one kindness. They keep my heart soft. I always want my heart to be soft. I always want to let people in.

I have a lot of gratitude for the doctors and nurses. They took extra time with me and didn't treat me like I was dumb. There is so much to be grateful for.

If you look for the tender mercies, you'll find them.

We're not going to change the world through war. We're going to do it through love. That's how love conquers. It wins people's hearts with kindness.

The connections you make and people that are good—there are way more of them than those that hate. That's the part I'm grateful for. Ben and I both see the goodness of the world.

Feel what you feel. Name it, and then you can let go. If you don't feel it and don't name it, it's going to come back and bite you. I'm grateful for that perspective.

Feel the grief, sadness, anger, bitterness. Once you've done it, you can let it go. You have to feel. You can't not feel. You'll end up hurting yourself if you don't feel.

Then, look at all the gifts that come.

- I will choose faith.
- I will choose hope.
- I will not be bitter.
- Every day, I looked for the small miracles.
- I am grateful for medical miracles.
- I am grateful for the Vietnam vets.
- I am grateful for the support of family and friends.
- One day at a time.
- Heavenly Father is carrying you.
- Let people in.
- Love will change the world.
- I am grateful for a soft heart.
- I am grateful for tender mercies.

Ben is doing well. He's found peace in his life. He's getting ready to snowboard this winter. He's working with the national disabilities board. Some of the people he trains with will go on to be in the Paralympics. He has always liked this kind of thing. He started working out with the team a couple of months ago. The healing process isn't over, but Ben *is* healing.

CHAPTER 12

Grief and Disconnected Feelings

*We are like puzzle pieces who are perfectly
suited to make a giant picture together, but
we are assembling ourselves in the dark.*
—Vironika Tugaleva, *The Love Mindset*

When we have experienced significant tragedy, we may think, *I just have
to keep going,* or, *I'm supposed to be strong for others.* Not taking time for
feeling and grief work leads us to separate ourselves from our emotions.

This disconnect can happen without our even thinking about it. A
friend's wife of thirty years died one Thursday. The funeral was Saturday. He came to church on Sunday and went back to work—business
as usual—on Monday. He took no time for himself just to be with his
emotions. He kept going with life as if nothing had ever happened.

What kind of sentiments does this incident bring to your mind?
Sorrow surfaces for me. I couldn't help but wonder, *Did he miss his
wife? Did he really love her?* It's sad for me to think of her looking down

from heaven and watching him not miss a beat when she's gone.

This good husband has omitted the grieving process, or maybe he's grieving internally. Was my friend afraid to allow the light of his dear wife to remain in his heart? I will probably never know. He's a private person and may be involved in solitary grief.

Maybe he wanted to keep his emotions inside, thinking to protect his children and grandchildren. Perhaps he did his grieving in private—a little at a time—as he carried on with his daily life. Maybe he's uncomfortable with emotion and has hidden it deep inside. It could be that his loss seemed so overwhelming that he didn't dare release his feelings for fear they would completely engulf him.

We'll never know the reason for how this husband and many others behave in the face of loss, but research published in the *Journal of Psychosomatic Research* has shown that suppressing emotions may increase the risk of dying from heart disease and certain forms of cancer.

After the death of a loved one, most of us want to keep precious memories alive. I believe that taking time to fully experience the loss is a memorial to them. But, we all heal in different ways. Your emotions may be close to the surface. You may cry a lot after a trauma. Others may not need to express many outward feelings. Some like to write in the privacy of their journal. Others need to talk and share with others. We are all different.

Give yourself permission to grieve according to your needs and express your feelings in a manner that is best for you.

As a child, Sam had been told by his father to "gut it up" whenever Sam's emotions surfaced. Sam spent his young life hiding his feelings. When his mother died, Sam's father said, "Men don't cry. Gut it up."

His grandmother came to care for Sam and his younger brother, but she died two years later when Sam was only ten. Sam didn't cry. The family dog died several months after that from cancer. Sam gulped back his tears and helped his father dig a grave in the backyard.

After graduating from college, Sam and his best friend, Jason, took sales jobs with a company in Salt Lake City. Jason was killed that winter in a skiing accident. A snowmobile plowed him down while he was cross-country skiing.

Sam was devastated, though he tried to "gut it up" as usual. But he couldn't eat. He couldn't sleep. His racing heart made him feel like he was having a heart attack. After spending all night in the emergency room, the doctor told him his heart was fine but suggested that he get involved in some grief therapy after his friend's death.

Sam sat in my office bouncing his leg and rubbing the back of his neck.

He reported the particulars of the skiing accident with no specific emotion.

I asked if there had been any other deaths in his past. He went on to tell about his mother, grandmother, and beloved dog. His leg bounced even faster.

Recognizing his intense anxiety, I chose to leave off with the questions until after doing some mindfulness and relaxation exercises, beginning with drawing his attention to his toes and working up his body to his head.

I asked him to be aware of his breathing. If thoughts came into his mind, he was to float them into the light and be mindful again of his breath.

Once he was relaxed, I asked him to be aware of his body, to notice the feelings in his body and extremities.

"I feel tension in my arms and legs," he told me. "But there is a heaviness in my body. My abdomen has weight in it. Maybe pressure in my heart area." He sat with these feelings and embraced them, but he couldn't think where they came from.

As his therapy progressed, he created a wise mentor. He discussed his body feelings with his mentor. The guide suggested that maybe they had to do with his father's demands that he bury his feelings when his mother died. Sam hugged himself and cried.

He spent some time recalling memories of his mother, visualizing the fun times they had together, the favorite foods they shared together, her teaching him to ride a bike.

He did the same with his grandmother and his dog.

Each time he checked in with his body, some of the heaviness was gone. The pressure in his heart changed to an expanding feeling of love. His body, as a whole, became more relaxed, and the racing-heart anxiety attacks diminished.

Sam recorded his emotions about the loss of his friend and those of his childhood in a journal. He began to find a more positive focus in life. Mindfulness and creative visualization had helped him come to know himself.

As Sam reconnected with his feelings, he reported that he found more pleasure in life. When his sessions ended, I suggested that he continue his meditation. He expanded is daily introspection to include a greater awareness of his surroundings and to take pleasure in them. He shared this list of mindful experiences:

- Savor the food I eat.
- Be aware of the softness of my pillow.
- Smell the aroma of hot coffee.
- Feel the warm sun on my back.
- Find pleasure of the wind blowing my hair when I drive down the road.

If we disconnect from our feelings, we are missing part of ourselves. Life is a journey to include our appreciation of the beauty and joy around us. If you ignore the difficult emotions, you limit your awareness of the beautiful ones. Meditation focuses on the awareness of our being and can bring positive energy into our lives. Our living will be enriched if we take advantage of this process.

Look at your own experience. Do you discount your own feelings? Are they hidden inside? Take a little time to write your feelings here. If complete privacy is important to you, take a notebook and write your thoughts, feelings, and emotions as you read. When you have recorded the things you would like, you may keep the notebook for further reference or destroy it as you wish.

_____

_____

_____

_____

_____

Summary

When you have experienced the loss of a significant other in your life, take time to be with your sadness. Use your mindfulness and creative visualization to facilitate this process. Meditation is a way to reconnect with our feelings when we have become disengaged.

Allow yourself to enjoy memories of a loved one who is gone as a tribute to them. Connect with your feelings and find ways to keep that connection with life alive.

Commitment

- If you find you are disconnected from your feelings, take time to reconnect.
- Grieve the loss you have separated yourself from.
- Spend some time each day connecting with your present self.
- Enjoy the beauty of your surroundings each day.

CHAPTER 13

Nightmares

*My sleep wasn't peaceful, though. I have
the sense of emerging from a world of dark,
haunted places where I traveled alone.*
—Suzanne Collins, *Mockingjay*

Nightmares are fairly common after a tragedy. They are the body's
way of telling us to pay attention and listen. They can also be a way of
working through traumatic experiences. At times, they are the result
of unresolved grief issues. The reasons for nightmares will be as varied
as the individuals experiencing them. Whatever the problem, listen
to the overarching message of your dreams, and set your life in order
accordingly.

In my past work with children, nightmares usually came as a result of
fear. It was very therapeutic for them to rewrite the dream with a positive
ending. I have used this technique with the adults I have worked with
as well, and it was healing for them also.

As a therapist, I could suggest endings to the dreams, but the suggestions were not nearly as restorative as the ideas the clients came up with
themselves. This seemed to have a deeper therapeutic impact.

I used the following procedure with children as well as adults:

1. Keep a written or picture journal of the dreams.
2. Bring the journal to therapy.
3. Brainstorm different endings.
4. Choose the positive finish that best fits each specific dream.
5. When you wake with a nightmare, take a few minutes in mindfulness to calm and comfort yourself.
6. Apply your resolution. Allow your mind to rest with it. Feel the positive peaceful energy that resonates from it.
7. Sleep comfortably.

Kayla, age seven, came to therapy because she was experiencing nightmares. She had just lost her grandmother. The two of them had been very close, spending every afternoon together after school. I asked Kayla what she would do when school was over now that her grandmother was gone. She explained that she would stay with the neighbor girl until her mother got off work.

Kayla said she was friends with the girl next door, and she would have a good time at her house, but she liked being with her grandmother better because her grandmother always read her stories as soon as Kayla finished her homework.

In her nightmare, Kayla was alone—always running after her grandmother, but never able to catch up with her. Kayla's mother said Kayla would wake up crying and frantic because her grandmother was out of reach.

I asked Kayla to draw a picture of the dream. In the picture, her grandmother was running away, but her face was turned toward Kayla. The drawing showed Kayla with no arms, indicating her feeling of helplessness.

Then I asked Kayla to draw a happy ending to her dream. She did, illustrating herself and her grandmother sitting on the sofa, reading their favorite books. I asked Kayla to draw herself giving her grandmother a hug and telling her thanks for all the reading they had done together.

I then suggested to Kayla that the two of them could read books together whenever Kayla wanted. All Kayla had to do was put the picture of them reading books in her mind. She and her grandmother could read as often as they wanted. Kayla left the session happy, and the nightmares never reoccurred.

We might all find ourselves in Kayla's position from time to time. This simple treatment method for rewriting our nightmares aids us in returning to a restful sleep pattern.

But what about those whose dreams are a product of horrific disasters? Even though many of us were not affected personally by the 9/11 terrorist attack, we all experienced an emotional impact of that tragedy.

Researchers Dr. Ernest Hartmann and Tyler Brezler from Tufts University in Boston, Massachusetts, published a study in the journal *Sleep* in 2008. This research project had begun before the 9/11 attack happened. Participants in this ongoing study had recorded ten dreams before 9/11. Then, right after 9/11, they were asked to journal ten more dreams. The results indicated that even though none of the contributors had a friend or relative involved in the World Trade Center attacks, there was a significant increase in nightmares (dreams involving some kind of an attack) among the participants. The authors of this study believe that dreams reflect the distress of our daily lives (in this case, anxiety concerning lack of security).

The study was designed to test the relationship between trauma and dreams. No further work was done to see if rewriting the dreams helped resolve the nightmares.

Even though the dream study participants did not have family and acquaintances connected to this tragic experience, it still affected them. Those of us who are exposed to trauma like this—even if it's from a distance—are affected. We can rewrite our dreams in the way we feel best.

Monica's grandmother survived a Nazi death camp. As a child, she listened to her grandmother's story over and over again. Monica was a young adult when her grandmother passed away. She missed her grandmother but was happy she was in heaven, a better place.

Monica married and the couple had a son. But by the time their son was in high school, the marriage fell apart when her husband had an affair and left the country. Just after their boy entered college, he was hit by a stray bullet in a gang shooting and killed.

After her son's death, Monica's nightmares became so intense she was afraid to go to sleep at night. She dreamed about being locked in a building with wooden bunks, filled with emaciated bedmates who had lots of fleas. She recognized the images from her grandmother's stories but couldn't understand why her dreams were of her grandmother's death camp experiences and not her son.

She came to therapy, concerned about the content of her dreams and panicked that she would lose her job because she was getting no rest. We talked about her being abandoned by everyone in her family. But she wasn't ready to look at that until she could get some sleep and maintain a consistent work schedule. She was completely focused in solving her nightmare puzzle. (And rightfully so; we have to be able to sleep if we are to function in daily life.)

I taught her about mindfulness and creative visualization. After she began her meditation process, I asked her to find a wise mentor inside.

She and her mentor discussed her dreams. The mentor suggested Monica create a memorial scholarship fund for her son. Monica had already planned to do this but had put it off until she could solve her nightmare problem.

"Being afraid to sleep at night is ruining my life," she said.

I strongly urged her to listen to her internal guide. Finally, she relented and set up the funding for the scholarship. A program at the local community college was held in her son's honor to advertise the scholarship. That very night, she slept soundly. The nightmares were gone.

Monica couldn't believe it. She told me in her next session that she thought it was odd that in her nightmares the childhood fears of her youth overshadowed the real present-day issue. Those fears had been hidden away—unnoticed until another tragedy triggered them.

I am always humbled and amazed at the wisdom we hold inside us. I found it such a privilege to be invited into the inner workings of my clients. The healing energy is deep within all of us if we will only access it. This story is a reminder for us to look inside for answers.

Summary

Nightmares are the body's way of telling us to listen. They are, at times, a product of unresolved personal and family issues. They can be the result of stress in the event of a natural disaster or terrorist attack.

When you experience bad dreams, take time to journal them. Listen to their message and look at your life to set things in order as per their meaning. Keep a dream journal, brainstorm positive endings, and choose the best one. When you wake in the night, apply your positive ending to the dream and allow your mind to feel its peace. If you feel the need to work with your internal mentor, do so and act on your conclusions. Like Monica, you can choose to follow through, refusing to let the nightmares to limit you.

Use the techniques we've discussed here if your dreams are troubling you. Begin keeping a dream journal. Brainstorm different endings to your dreams. Use your internal guide to help you choose a positive solution that seems to fit best. Then, when you wake from a nightmare, take a few minutes in a mindfulness exercise to calm and comfort yourself. Apply your resolution and allow your mind to feel the peace of this positive energy. Then sleep comfortably.

Commitment

- Keep a dream journal.
- Look for the past and present issues the dreams address.
- Write positive endings to your nightmares.
- Apply them to your dreams.
- Order your life, according to the message of your dreams.

CHAPTER 14

Facing Fears

No one ever told me that grief felt so like fear.
—C. S. Lewis, *A Grief Observed*

The death of a beloved partner is devastating at best. At worst, it can be crippling, sending the grieving partner into complete inactivity. Facing the fear of continuing without your loved one, or of grieving the loss of a spouse, can be an overwhelming mountain to climb.

Fear has many faces. Here are several suggestions that may apply to you (or you may write your own):

- I'm afraid of being overwhelmed by my feelings.
- I'm afraid of hurting too much to look at my loss.
- I'm afraid that I can't function without my spouse.

_____

_____

_____

_____

We assume that in order to let go of our grief, we need to reiterate the details surrounding a death—face the trauma. At times, this may be exactly what is needed, but there are other times when a person feels so devastated by the loss that a dose of positive emotional strength must come first.

Upbeat memories can fortify not only a grieving partner but also the entire family. If a family or an individual can increase positive energy flow, it will allow them to look at incidents surrounding the death without falling to pieces.

Positive recollections can strengthen grieving individuals so they will be able to face their fears.

Look at your own situation. If you feel you can't address the details surrounding your grief, spend some time strengthening yourself before you address the tragedy.

Here's the story of a family I had in therapy. The widower (and father) wasn't emotionally strong enough to look at his wife's passing and the details that accompanied it. First, he had to strengthen himself before he could address that issue.

Walter lost his wife of fifteen years to a degenerative muscular disease. She suffered a slow, agonizing death. Walter was distraught when she finally passed. His mother came to take care of the three children, ages ten, seven, and five, while he was at work—but Walter couldn't get out of bed to go to work.[1]

Since Walter was depressed and couldn't even go to work, his mother suggested he and the rest of the family go to therapy so they could get on with their lives. When they came in for counseling, there was an overwhelming sense of sadness surrounding all of them. Walter sat down and put his head in his hands.

---

[1] Seek therapy if you see the following signs of depression: depressed mood, diminished interest in life, significant weight loss, insomnia, restlessness or fatigue, feelings of worthlessness, inability to concentrate, and recurring thoughts of death or suicide.

During the "get acquainted" part of the session, I learned from Jane, age ten, that she wanted to go to a movie with the family. She complained that they never did anything together anymore. Dad needed something to think about besides how lonely and sad he was. The two younger boys wanted their father to take them to a baseball game.

I suggested to Walter that all three children were trying to help him get back into life.

He looked up, smiled, and nodded his head.

I asked them if there was anything happy going on in this family. No one answered. The two boys looked at Dad and put their heads down.

Jane said, "That's the problem. We are never happy now. When Mother was alive, we laughed and did things together. Even when she was sick, we still had some fun times. Now that she's gone, everyone is sad."

"Can we take a few minutes and remember happy times with your mother?" I asked.

Each of the children, in turn, related memories of a picnic in the park, telling jokes while playing a board game, reading stories before bed, making blueberry pancakes on Saturday mornings, and several other incidents.

Walter didn't offer any memories. He just listened, but he took his head out of his hands.

"I want to be happy like we were," said the five-year-old.

"Good idea," I said. "Let's have a family meeting and see if we can come up with some ideas of how to do that."

We all pulled our chairs into a circle and added a chair for Mother.

Walter had a picture of Mother in his wallet, so I had the five-year-old put the picture on the empty chair. He did so with great ceremony. Then, he turned to his dad. "Mother wants you to take us to the ball game."

Jane laughed. "Good try."

Walter sat up a little straighter. "I want to have happy times, too. I know I need to get going. I will try."

"Ball game," said the five-year-old.

"Okay," said Walter.

The boys cheered.

We outlined several other activities for the week, and Walter promised to participate.

This family began to function again with a somewhat limited level of activity, but at least they were going again. There were still no soccer practices or ballet lessons, but Walter went to work every day and played ball with the kids at the park in the evenings.

We continued to hold family meetings with the empty chair. Each of the children took turns talking for Mother, giving suggestions and telling her thoughts.

With the family's ego strength in better shape, I suggested that we talk about missing Mother. We set the empty chair for this session as we had done before. Each of the children shared their feelings of loneliness.

"But it's not as sad as it was," said the seven-year-old. "We can talk to her anytime we have a meeting."

"But it's not the same," said Jane.

"No, it's not," I said, "and it never will be." I shared the death of my father with the family. "Even though I talk to my dad, it's not the same."

I asked Walter to come in the next week alone and bring a letter to his wife.

In the letter, he told her he felt guilty because he couldn't keep her alive. He had prayed fervently for her to get well, and she still died. Maybe God ignored his plea. He told God he would rather die than her, but God didn't listen. He said the pain was so great, he didn't know if he could live. The only thing that kept him going was his children.

I put an empty chair across from his and asked him to change seats. Would he tell me what his wife's response to his letter would be?

He was visibly shaking when he moved to the other chair, but he continued with the exercise. Though he was by this time sobbing, Walter told me that she would say she loved him, God was there, and He was listening. He smiled and chuckled through his tears. "She would tell me she's glad I'm off my backside, and she's happy I'm taking care of the kids."

I asked him to sit with an image of her next to him. Could they continue to work together to raise the children—only in a little different way? Could he discuss things with her like he was doing right now?

He looked up. "I know I've been scared to face all this. I guess I was afraid I couldn't do this alone. I still love her so much; I don't want her to be gone. Tonight, I can feel her close to me."

We talked again about the death of my father, and I told him that my father was always close when I needed to talk.

"I hope I can do this," he said. "I hope."

The family continued sessions, allowing the children to write letters to their mother and then pen her response. (The boys drew her pictures, but we'll talk more about art therapy in a later chapter.) The family decided to plant several pine trees along the end of their backyard in honor of their mother. She had wanted them there, but Walter hadn't gotten around to planting them.

Slowly, the family began to recover. But Jane was right. It would never be the same. Her mother would miss the excitement of Jane's first date, and she wouldn't be at Jane's wedding. Substitute people would be there, and Jane could talk to her mother and tell her everything. It would be okay, but not the same.

I encouraged the family to continue to include their mother in journaling and visualizations. Whenever they had a special family celebration, they could add memories of their mother and think about what she would be doing to participate in this festive occasion.

Jane felt comforted, knowing she could talk to her mother any time she wished to discuss problems she was having or difficult decisions facing her. Her mother became an internal guide, being a sounding board for Jane as she continued through life.

Walter kept a close bond with his wife, sharing with her the joys and sorrows of life. He said that he and his wife would continue to have a close relationship—only in a different way now.

Summary

After the death of a loved one, fear over the loss can be overwhelming. As the bereaved, you may need to spend time focusing on positive memories until you feel strong enough to face the loss. Give yourself permission to define and address your fears as you are able.

Like Walter and his children, fortify yourself with the support of family and friends and memories of good times. Give voice to what a lost loved one would want for you, and include them in discussions, decisions, and special times. As you embrace the good things, past and present, the fear of grief won't be insurmountable.

Commitment

- Practice daily life skills.
- Reminisce about happy times.
- Define your fears.
- Allow yourself to face them as you are ready.
- Use an empty chair to talk to your loved one.
- Write letters to them, telling them your feelings.

CHAPTER 15

Anger

Anything that works against you can also work for you once you understand the Principle of Reverse.
—Maya Angelou, *I Know Why the Caged Bird Sings*

Anger is a secondary emotion, usually covering the primary emotions of fear, guilt, pain, or hopelessness. It is one of the stages of grief defined in chapter 3:

- Denial
- Anger
- Bargaining
- Shame
- Depression
- Acceptance

These stages of grief are listed in an order, but they aren't necessarily experienced in that order. Our feelings cannot be categorized. We feel them as they come.

If we feel, we can heal.

Anger can appear at any stage of our grieving. It's important to talk about anger because most of us are taught from an early age not to be angry. Many people spend much of their time denying this feeling and thinking of it as *bad*.

Anger can be a positive emotion if we use it to help us. Anger is a signal for us to set our boundaries. I can feel angry inside when someone steps on my toes. If this happens, I don't need to rage at the person who stepped on my toes. I can ask them, in a kind way, to get off my foot and go on with life.

Anger at myself is a sign of guilt. It's a signal that I may have made a mistake. Sometimes, I do things that are not as I would have them. I want to accept my imperfections and look at my behavior to order my life so that I feel peaceful.

Anger can also be a critical, judgmental way of thinking. Have you ever been around someone who is constantly saying negative things about others—a person who never has anything good to say about anyone? This type of anger is adverse and destructive. When you find it to be part of your life, get rid of it. (See the chapter 23 for more about positive thinking.)

Anger can become a bond, helping us hold on to a deceased loved one. If you're angry at the doctor, the paramedics, the drunk driver, or your loved one, that helps you keep an anger bond with the one who has abandoned you.

We can either be bonded
in love or in anger.

Intense anger is an indication of the strong love we felt for the deceased. It is a sign of passionate grief—as strong as our passionate love.

Remember the dark hole of feelings we talked about in chapter 3? When we are overwhelmed with negative feelings, anger can be one way to climb out of that dark hole. It energizes us to hike up one rock after another until we are out of the hole. Anger turned outward will keep us from spiraling our anger inward, sending us into a state of depression.

Anger is part of the grief process. It can be a lifeline to pull us from an ocean of grief into the boat of healing. At times, it is a secondary emotion, covering our fear, pain, sadness, loneliness, and frustration when these primary emotions are just too painful to look at and feel.

To summarize, anger is:

- A signal that change is needed.
- A cover-up.
- A bond.
- A sign of love.
- A ladder.
- An antidepressant.

Note this in the following incident.

Danny, age ten, was an average student at school. During the fall, he got along pretty well with the other kids in his class. But in early January, when he came back to school after the holiday break, he began shoving the other kids. He stood too close to several of the girls and yelled at them to get out of his way. He was sullen and argumentative in the school counselor's office.

His teacher tried talking to him—helping him plan ahead and giving him small behavior goals. Nothing did any good. He was angry. A fistfight brought him into my office for counseling.

As I met with Danny's parents, the clarity of his situation unraveled itself. His parents were headed for a divorce. His father was leaving in two weeks. Danny's world as he had known it since birth was falling to pieces—his own personal tragedy. Underneath his anger was pain and fear and sadness.

Danny could see that his anger covered his fear concerning a new life. What would happen to him? Both his parents assured him that they would love him and care for him. Even though his life would be different, he would still have their support. Because his father was leaving, they decided on a plan to talk over Skype together a couple of times a week and visit as often as they could.

By the time Danny left therapy, he had a list of tools that he could use if he felt angry: separate himself to his bedroom, punch his pillow, kick a pile of dirty clothes, play basketball or soccer, and punch a duffel bag full of rags that hung in the garage.

Anger has been given a bad rap. These uses of anger are all good. Let it help you with understanding, and it will be the lifeline out of your grief. If you stay stuck in your lifeline, however, you can get tangled in the rope that will eventually strangle you. And if you see yourself descending into harmful behavior—any form of acting out that hurts others—your anger is a hindrance. Stop! Step back and look at your behavior. Find an outlet that will not harm those around you. Select a healthy way to release your anger that will not inflict pain on others.

So accept anger, use it as a vehicle to get through your grieving, and move on.

Malcolm was a local doctor. He was well known in his area of the Las Vegas valley and had a large, lucrative practice. He came for counseling about once a month to get what he called a tune-up. He liked to talk about his seven children, his wife, and ways to keep his family functioning in a healthy manner. He would come into each session, shake hands in greeting, sit down, cross his legs, put his wallet in his sock, and begin to talk.

As a hobby, Malcolm loved flying experimental airplanes. The desert of Nevada was a great place to investigate new designs and new machines. Once, he took his two older children with him—to the absolute terror of his wife. She said it was so dangerous that she didn't sleep for a week after the kids got home. He never took them again.

Malcolm and a friend tried out a new plane. The weather was rainy, but they went anyway. The aircraft went down and they were both killed.

Malcolm's wife, Alice, came in for several sessions after his death. "I'm angry at him for leaving me. Yes, I have enough money to raise the children and send them to college. But I have to do it by myself. We were a good team and now we're not." She sighed.

I asked her to be with her anger. Allow herself to feel it.

She talked it through. She journaled it. She had a good girlfriend she met for lunch whom she could unload her feelings on. She got a punching bag for the garage. Their teenage son was angry also. Most all Malcolm's kids took a turn with the bag.

Alice held on to her anger for a while before she let it go. She said, "I need to keep it for a while. It gives me the energy to care for these grieving children. There are eight of us here!"

She eventually let it go and forgave Malcolm. "At times, he seemed like just a little kid in a man's body. I love him for that."

How did Alice get through her anger?

She talked.

She journaled her feelings.

She met with a friend and grieved.

She did the body work to vent her feelings.

Alice grieved as was best for her. How about you?

Use your mindful moments to become aware of your anger.

- Does your anger have a purpose?
- What is underneath your anger?
- Is anger your friend right now?
- Could it become your enemy?
- What is the difference? Give an example.
- What is your plan for letting it go?

Letting Go

Remember, thinking creates our feelings.

1. Spend some mindful moments becoming aware of your anger. Know that it has been your friend. Feel it. Embrace it.
2. Create a plan for releasing your negative feelings:
   a. Punch a bag.
   b. Scream into your pillow.
   c. Listen to soothing music.
   d. Go to the gym and work out your feelings.
3. Surround yourself with good friends. Ask them to hold up an emotional mirror for you. Give them permission to tell you when you are being strangled by your lifeline. Take some time away from your feelings by having fun with friends. Watch a movie, go paint-balling, play racquetball.
4. Rather than being *against* someone who has angered you, be *for* yourself. Spend some time in your daily meditation. Listen to your wise mentor. Do some good things for yourself.
5. Put yourself in the place of the person you are angry with. Empathize with them. Alice knew Malcolm loved flying his planes.

6. Say goodbye to your anger and grieve your loss at the primary emotional level—which means face your fear, pain, sadness, or whatever other feelings are covered by your anger. Spend mindful moments with these feelings and release them.

7. Find some way to give service to others. Each day, set a goal to make the world a better place in some small way. Even if I only tell a neighbor I like her haircut, it's adding light to the world.

Summary

Sometimes, anger gets a bad rap. But look at the good that can come from your anger. It can be your protector, bond you to your loved one, and help you get through your initial grief. Embrace it and feel it. Find some physical exercise to help you release your feelings. Listen inside about how to let go. Spend time with friends to give yourself a break. Feel your primary emotions and then let go. Give some service to make the world a better place.

Commitment

- Meditate daily with your mindfulness.
- Feel your anger.
- Workout daily.
- Surround yourself with good friends.
- Feel your pain and sadness.
- Give service to others.

CHAPTER 16

Forgiveness

There were many dark moments when my faith in humanity was sorely tested, but I would not and could not give myself up to despair. That way lay defeat and death.
—Nelson Mandela, *Long Walk to Freedom*

No one is born hating another person because of the color of his skin, or his background, or his religion. People must learn to hate, and if they can learn to hate, they can be taught to love, for love comes more naturally to the human heart than its opposite.
—Nelson Mandela, *Long Walk to Freedom*

There are many great leaders and humanitarians that have lived on this earth that I admire, but to me, Nelson Mandela is one of the greatest. After twenty-seven years in prison—many of those years with harsh treatment—he walked free with compassion and love in his heart.

Researchers at Johns Hopkins University found that forgiveness can lower your risk of heart attack, improve your sleep, and reduce pain, blood pressure, and anxiety. Lingering anger can put you in a fight-or-flight mode that may increase your risk of heart disease, depression, and apprehension. Aex Harris nd colleagues found in studies conducted at Stanford that forgiveness significantly reduces stress and depression with an increase of physical vitality.

When the young teenager sped angrily down the road, ran a stop sign, and killed my father, I felt victimized. I was bitter. But I had no one with whom I could talk though my anger. My mother never said anything negative about that angry young man, and I don't know how she felt because we never talked about it.

In my early years, I was angry and resentful. The negative feelings festered inside me like a raw and bleeding wound.

After my father died, he and I had long conversations about life through visualizations. In my mind, I could tell him everything, but I didn't really have a father living with me. I didn't feel comfortable around boys. I felt inadequate and knew no one would really like me. As I worked with a therapist during my graduate program, I became aware that I had developed a childhood belief that men would abandon me. I sat with that pain. I embraced it.

Anger was not an asset for me anymore. I had kept it with me over the years to cover my pain and sadness, but I couldn't move on as long as I held it. I wasn't a little girl that needed a daddy to protect and care for her anymore. That time was past. I was an adult and needed to mentor myself. I needed to let that anger go by embracing forgiveness. When there is no longer a positive payoff for your anger, let it go and allow forgiveness into your life.

Remember Alice in the preceding chapter? She held on to her anger at first because it gave her energy to get herself and her children through the initial grief that surrounded them. When she and her children moved beyond that place, she began to release her anger.

I became aware of my pain and wanted to find a way out. Through creative visualization, I used my father as a wise mentor. He listened to my anger, loneliness, feelings of abandonment, and childhood fears.

As I journaled and talked and cried, I let go of the animosity inside me. A burden lifted off me. It was as if I walked out of the fog into sunlight.

This process wasn't about me forgiving that angry teenager at all. It was about me letting go of my resentment and feelings from the past. When I finally felt clear of my anger, I found so many gifts that had come from this experience that I was overwhelmed.

I began to keep a thankfulness journal. I had as many pages of gratitude entries as I had about my black anger. Here are a few:

- My pain has refined me with a maturity that I couldn't have received any other way.
- I know the path from childhood dependence to that of self-compassion and love.
- My life wasn't perfect, but I knew the way out of my black hole. I can help myself.
- Because of the pain I have suffered, I can empathize with others.
- Hurt and sadness had been my friends. They polished me.
- I have a depth of understanding that helps me mentor myself and others.
- I have found a daily meditation process that brings me peace.

My plan for peace:
- I meditate daily.
- I spend time with my visualizations.
- I use positive self-talk to eradicate my victim thinking.
- I find time for spiritual focus each day.
- I give some kind of service to others every day.

Set a plan to find your own forgiveness.
1. Set a goal. The resentment and anger you are holding is only hurting you and no one else. Where do you see yourself in a year, two years, five years? Do you feel stuck?
2. Develop empathy. One of the keys to forgiveness is to put yourself in the place of the person you are angry with. Can you empathize with them? What would it be like to look at the world through their eyes?
3. Let go of expectations. We all have expectations of how others should respond to us or how they should behave. Let go of those. Whoever wronged you may not apologize. They may not even know that they wronged you. In the case of the young teen that killed my father, he went on with his life. I was the one who carried

the cancer of resentment inside me. It wasn't about him changing. It was about me letting go of my negativity.

4. Internalize forgiveness. Don't forgive just because God says you should. Really forgive. There's an Alcoholics Anonymous statement that says, "Let go and let God." Put things in the hands of your higher power. (See chapter 34 for more on spirituality.)

5. Write your feelings. Journal an angry letter to your perpetrator and then destroy the letter. I always let my clients choose how they would do that. After they wrote, they burned the letter, shredded it, stamped it into the mud, or released it in a bottle into the ocean. Decide what will be therapeutic for you.

6. Forgive yourself. Also remember to write a letter of forgiveness to yourself. Many times, we harbor anger toward ourselves for the way we have handled a situation or the things we have done.

Finding peace inside is a habit we need to develop. Every time a judgmental thought comes into your head, sit with it in a mindful meditation. Embrace this thinking. It has kept you safe in the past, but it isn't working for you now. Give it a color. A shape. Turn it sideways. Thank it for being part of your life. Float it off into a cloud.

Notice something good in your present surroundings—like the light coming in the window, the sunshine around you, the soft touch of your clothing. Think of a good thing that happened to you in the past few days. Smile at the pleasant feeling. Remember a caring act from a friend or family member. Be grateful for the good in the world. You are part of it.

_____

_____

_____

_____

The weak can never forgive. Forgiveness
is an attribute of the strong.
—Mahatma Gandhi, *All Men Are Brothers*

Summary

Harboring resentment and anger is harmful to your health. It can contribute to heart disease, depression, and anxiety. Forgiveness is the medicine for healing. Establish a plan to let go of your resentment. Set a goal, focusing on where you would like to be in a few years. Put yourself in the place of the other person. What would your behavior be if you were in their shoes? Let go of expectations concerning other's behavior. Shift your focus to positive things. Don't forgive because you think you have to or for the sake of the other person; forgive because it will be a blessing to you.

Commitment

- Take inventory of your resentful feelings.
- Write an angry letter and then destroy it.
- Find peace by noticing something good in your present surroundings.
- Think of a good thing that happened to you in the past few days.
- Enjoy that pleasant feeling.
- Remember the caring act of a friend.
- Be grateful for the good in your world.

CHAPTER 17

Letter to Your Loved One

"There is no death, daughter. People die only when we forget them," my mother explained shortly before she left me. "If you can remember me, I will be with you always."
—Isabel Allende, *Eva Luna*

Letter-writing can be a powerful tool in our healing process. Sometimes, letting go can only come when aided by an exchange of letters with a loved one who has passed on. James Pennebaker, in *Writing to Heal*, notes that this process can reduce stress and enhance the mood of the letter writer. The Center for Growth in Philadelphia reports that those who wrote letters or even journaled had a better outlook on life and better physical health.

Take some time before you begin to write to think about what you want to say. Let your feelings guide the letter-writing process. If you need to pen an angry letter to your loved one for leaving you, start there. If you are upset at the circumstances that took him or her away, begin at that point. Write not only about the particulars of your situation but also explore the process of letting go and embracing forgiveness.

You can begin the letter with memories, feelings, or just sharing what's happening in your life right now.

Here are some beginning sentences, or write your own possible beginnings:

- I miss you because . . .
- I'm so lonely . . .
- I'm angry at you for leaving me . . .
- Life is harder now . . .
- I wonder where you are . . .
- Are you near enough to know my thoughts . . . ?

If you aren't ready to write to your deceased loved one, you can also write to your future self, your family, or a caring confidant. Lynne's husband died of cancer just after the holidays. She wrote a letter to share her feelings. Here are a few of her thoughts:

> When he first passed away, I was positive that I wouldn't live more than a year, so I basically waited to die. Morbid but true. Now I'm five years out, still here, and amazed that time passes so quickly, and still feels like forever. It was several years before I didn't cry every day. And then, when I didn't, I felt guilty. We loved to travel and visited many states and countries and shared many beautiful things. Now when I travel, I bounce between missing him and sharing the experience with him. He comes and goes. He drops by from time to time, unexpectedly, and it is painful joy. It's always fleeting, and that's probably a good thing because when it happens, I'm pretty sure I don't breathe. I mostly live with the warm assurance that I have a beautiful, secret companionship that only I know about. It's like a promise, and it's warm.

When you've lost a loved one, grieving is a process that doesn't happen in a day or a year. Life goes on, and we learn to adjust and live a new way, but the sadness never leaves us. Many times, we keep the grief in our hearts, not wanting to share. Letters are a way of letting our family know the precious connection we have experienced. Lynne's letter is a great family legacy to be passed on for generations.

Amy came into therapy depressed. She had lost interest in life and could hardly get out of bed in the morning. Overwhelming feelings of worthlessness kept her from going to work each day. She had used so many sick days, she was in danger of losing her job.

She missed her boys' high school ball games. She couldn't get herself out of bed to go four-wheeling with the family.

Amy broke down in tears as she shared her story. Fourteen years ago, her daughter, Julie, had drowned in the bathtub as a young child. Amy had punished herself for years over the death. She had left Julie in only three inches of water for just a minute to answer the phone. When she came back, Julie was gone. They called the paramedics, but Julie couldn't be revived.

When her boys were in grade school, Amy kept up with all their activities—distracting herself from thinking of Julie. But now that the boys were more independent and didn't need as much of her time, haunting thoughts and guilt oppressed her. Amy's repressed emotions would not be held in any longer. They demanded attention. It was time to address them.

All she could think about was Julie—how she would be starting high school. Amy and Julie could be shopping together and seeing movies together. Julie was missing life, and it was all Amy's fault.

Amy had involved herself with her family when the kids were young, but as they grew older, she focused more and more on her lost daughter, separating herself from her living family.

Amy's pent-up emotions that had been hidden for so many years surfaced. Inconsolable grief seemed to envelop her entire being. She sobbed out her pain. She talked through her sadness. She journaled her sorrow, and she sketched her misery.

She did some creative visualization work, making an internal park where she and Julie could spend time together. But she didn't seem able to connect with Julie. Amy felt stuck. "I feel too guilty to even face her."

I asked Amy to write a letter to Julie, apologizing to her for leaving her alone in the bathtub and letting Julie know how much she missed her.

Amy spent a lot of time composing the letter. She told Julie how lonely she was without her and outlined all the things they could do if they were together. She told Julie how sorry she was and that it was her fault Julie wasn't enjoying life right now. Amy also let Julie know that she loved her dearly and was excited for them to be together in heaven. Amy felt some peace after writing the letter—but not enough.

Then I asked Amy to write Julie's response to the letter. She struggled to do so.

Julie told her mother how much she loved her. She was also sad they were separated. But she forgave Julie and told her not to punish herself anymore. Julie loved her mother and went on to say she wanted to spend time with her mother in the park. Would Amy come and be with her and hold her and love her?

From then on, Amy meditated every day with Julie in their park. They held and loved each other. Amy's depression slowly lifted. She spent more time with her living family as well as with Julie.

The letter-writing facilitated the creative visualization when Amy was stuck. Amy's guilt kept her from being able to establish a good relationship with her daughter. As she let go of her self-reproach, she could move forward.

Julie's letter helped Amy find her self-compassion. Allowing ourselves to be less than perfect is a lifelong journey—a journey toward peace.

Sit to write your own letter now. Here are some writing prompts to get you started.

- After the (write the incident that happened) I felt . . .
- I think about . . .
- I wish . . .
- Your influence in my life . . .
- When I think about . . .
- Remember the holiday we . . .
- The things I miss about you are . . .
- Memories of . . . haunt me because . . .

Summary

Letter-writing can be a powerful tool in helping us articulate our feelings. It can be one of the most powerful methods available to us. Letter-writing can release pent-up emotions and lead us toward a happier, healthier life.

Write letters to your loved one but also imagine what your loved one would write back to you. Opening up the communication can also free you to healthy understanding emotions.

Commitment

- Think about how you will begin a letter to your loved one.
- Outline some of the things you want to say.
- Spend as much time writing the letter as you need.
- Write a response from your loved one, telling you how they feel.

CHAPTER 18

Grief and the Creative Arts

Give sorrow words; the grief that does not speak whispers the o'erfrought heart and bids it break.
—William Shakespeare, *Macbeth* (IV, iii, 209–10)

When grief is brand-new—in its beginning stages—we can shut down, too heavy with sorrow to do anything. We may lack spontaneity and become closed off because of overwhelming sadness. In *Your Creative Brain*, Dr. Shelley Carson suggests that creativity is a way to heal our grief, but we may not be able to do this right after a tragedy. We may need to let a little time pass so that we become better acquainted with our grief. Then, our creativity can return and burst forth as a means of processing our passionate feelings.

Since individual emotions vary during periods of grieving, we must each find our own way to process sorrow. The use of art in any form as an expressive release will help us sit with our sadness, look at it, feel it, and process it. When creativity is used as a method of grieving, we participate in the artistic endeavors to understand and release our feelings, not to create something of beauty that will astound the world. Maybe we will astonish the world, but most likely not.

The focus of the art should be on the ongoing use of the medium and not necessarily the final product. All of the creative arts, including drawing, painting, sculpting, creating a memory quilt, practicing any form of handiwork, playing music, scrapbooking, writing the deceased's story, journaling, compiling your own story, acting, and dancing can be included in the healing process. They help us reach deep in our souls to find our authenticity.

Use a combination of any of these as you see fit or find another medium I haven't mentioned.

Because the brain records its trauma in its nonverbal area, art is a good means of expression since it doesn't take words to tell the story. The artistic endeavor can then begin to put the story to words so that the trauma might be processed by the verbal part of the brain.

A journal of emotions (i.e., a feeling journal) is a great place to begin. Gather paper in a variety of colors or use paint swatches. Study the colors carefully and assign an emotion to each hue. On the back pages of your journal, create a key for your colored emotions.

Each day when you meditate, record a page with your feelings in your paints or colored paper. You can leave the pages just as they are with the colors only or you can add drawings or pictures or doodles to every page as you wish.

Remember, you aren't making this journal as a prize pictograph. You are recording it for yourself to log your emotions of grief as the days go by.

Early in human history, the drum and flute were used to create ceremonies for the living and the dying: One drum beat represented the heartbeat of the person that had left this life. A second drum symbolized the living person—two hearts beating together. The two meld into one so that they might finish their dialogue and complete their grief, moving on to a new state of communication. This can be replicated by anyone wishing to create a ceremony that will lead to connection with a deceased loved one.

Music can be a powerful healer because of its strong effect on our emotions. Maybe you and your loved one had special music you listened to together. If you play an instrument, work out your feelings through melody. If your loved one belonged to a rock band, you might want them to perform at the funeral. Include the music that has a healing gift for you. Many of my clients felt a great release of their grief through music.

Dance is another artistic form that uses the body's large muscles to create. This is an excellent outlet because you have an artistic release as well as a good workout. Dance can be a form of solitary grief and a medium the entire community can participate in.

In the early years of this century, a Rwandan village heaped the skulls and bones of their dead into a cement mound with a tin roof overhead. The people were filled with sadness and hopelessness until the community gathered broken pottery shards and paint to create a fitting community memorial for the deceased. The village transformed their grief into beauty by honoring their dead. What a good way for a town, a group of friends, a church unit, or a family to grieve and honor a loved one who has left their midst.

Art can be individual and simple too. Nona, age five, had lost her father the year before. He was killed in a military skirmish in the Middle East. Her mother had a new serious relationship. Nona didn't know if she liked the man who would take the place of her father. The family came in to do some counseling to facilitate the blending process and help Nona feel comfortable with the new relationship. She drew a picture of herself playing at the park. She put two suns in the picture—indicating that she had two fathers now.

This picture gave us the opportunity to open up the discussion about the two fathers in her life. One would not replace the other. She took some time to be with her sadness at the loss of her biological father. Then she could move into the relationship with the new father in her life. She had the blessing of having two to love her instead of just one.

I was privileged to have some client-artists. One, an abuse survivor, worked through her feelings by creating intricate art designs on paper.

Coloring complex designs has become a popular art. There are creative sketches that you can color as part of your meditation or draw your own as part of your healing, as this client did.

Another client had been ritually abused in a Satanic cult. She created art during her healing process, but when she was about finished, her inner child asked her to draw one last painting as a memorial to the suffering she had been through. The chalk drawing was a large poster with a head. It had a stunning, eerie quality I will never forget.

After she shared the poster with me, her inner child was satisfied. She was at peace with life.

Collages can be a collection in any style the participant wishes. They can be made from anything—from magazine pictures to wild flowers or even pinecones from your local ecosystem. Draw a gratitude collage and include all the kindnesses that have been given you during your time of grief. Create a poster of all the cards you have received. Use your imagination. Think outside the box. What will mend your grief?

Carol grew up with a mother who liked to sew. When her mother died, she inherited the fabric scraps left over from all her childhood clothes. She decided to make a quilt from them as a memorial to her mother. She had thought she would use it on her bed during the winter months, reminding her of the warmth of her mother's love. But she couldn't bring herself to put it on the bed because she wanted everyone to see it. She found a place to hang it in her family room for all her children and grandchildren to admire—a memorial to her mother for everyone to enjoy.

Journaling has been discussed in the chapters on creative visualization, nightmares, anger, forgiveness, biography, positive thinking, and mantras. Create your own writing as is best for you. Other chapters have talked about writing letters to deceased loved ones. Children can draw pictures for loved ones and write stories about them as they wish.

The journaling process for me is a spontaneous one. I know I want to write something, but I don't know what I'm going to write about. I sit down with my journal and begin. Words seem to tumble onto the page. At first, the writing is scattered, and then the problem I'm writing about comes into focus. It's like looking through a camera lens and not quite knowing what the image is. Soon, however, the picture comes into focus, and I can see clearly. The problem has been externalized from my subconscious to the paper and I know myself better than I did a few minutes ago.

Another powerful grief medium is the written word in story form. Several children's books come to mind: *Missing May* by Cynthia Rylant, *Moon Over Manifest* by Clare Vanderpool, and *The One and Only Ivan* by Katherine Applegate. There are many good books about grief. I chose these three because an art medium is used in all of them for the grieving process. Literature is a wonderful way for all of us to escape from the moment and yet come to understand ourselves in the moment.

Creativity is a very personal journey. It comes from the heart and must be experienced by the heart. It is a very private process you can keep to yourself or share as you wish. Tap into your artistic experience to heal your grief. The gifts you will receive from it will bring you to experience your authenticity on a new level. Enjoy this new beginning.

Summary

When grief is new, heavy sorrow may keep you from your creativity. As you become better acquainted with your pain, find personal ways to release your feelings through imaginative processes. Allow yourself to explore developed talents or hidden ones. Create to bring your feelings into verbal awareness so that your story can be told.

Commitment

- Become acquainted with your grief.
- Explore ways to release your feelings through the creative process.
- Allow your creativity to bring your story to light.
- Share as you wish.
- Enjoy the new self-awareness you have discovered.

CHAPTER 19

Body Work and Grieving

*If we will be quiet and ready enough, we shall
find compensation in every disappointment.*
—Henry David Thoreau, *I to Myself*

Becoming comfortable with the change that's taken place after a tragic
incident—especially in the case of the death of a loved one—is a process
that takes time. Research as cited in the *Journal of Affective Disorders*
has shown that normal stress seems to linger when we are grieving. The
body can be slower to respond when everyday issues arise. So remember that this is a process and give yourself time to mourn at a pace that
works for you.

In chapter 10, we discussed body work concerning trauma—either
ongoing from childhood or because of an accident. In this chapter, the
circumstances are different. Instead of traumatization, your task is that
of looking at and processing grieving and loss.

Go back and review chapter 10, because there are many similarities to the body work in each scenario. The trauma may or may not be stored in your body, depending on the circumstances. But if you experienced the tragedy along with your lost loved one, then you will likely have your own body work to do along with the grief for your loss.

Sometimes, we don't know how to find the path to peace, but we keep searching.

I share my story and clients' stories to let you know the path to wholeness is as varied as the individuals walking that path. I hope that in reading these accounts, you understand your grief and find a new way for your relationship to continue beyond the grave.

Grieving is such an individual process. There is no right or wrong way to do it. We must all hunt to find the way that's best for us.

My grandmother died in our home at age ninety-nine. She was the joy of my life. After the death of my father (when I was six), we lived with my grandmother, and she took care of us while Mother went to school and worked. My grandmother was like a second parent in the home. She read to me every night before bed, taught me to cook, and showed me the fine art of homemaking. She helped me make my first dress. She loved to garden, and I worked alongside her.

Three years before her death, she needed significant help and came to live with me and my own family. She loved children and enjoyed playing games with our kids. She fit into the family almost like another child. When she died, I felt like I had lost one of my children. I wandered the house, distraught and full of anxiety and grief. I sat in the sun and tried to pull myself together. I couldn't.

I wasn't supposed to feel this way—others had emotions like this, but not me. (I can still see the little six-year-old inside me and her mistaken beliefs at my father's death.) I came to the realization that I had my own grief work to do.

Anxiety and sadness overwhelmed me. I couldn't just sit in the sun. I paced back and forth on the patio. That didn't help. I had to do something. I walked into the kitchen and decided to make bread just like my grandmother taught me. I had a bread mixer and could have let the machine whip it up in just a few minutes. But I decided to knead it by hand the way my grandmother first taught me.

As my arms and hands worked the dough, I began to cry, and I could feel some of my anxiety leave my body. My sadness lifted. It wasn't gone by any means, but it wasn't overwhelming like it had been.

The next few days, I made lots of bread. My husband and kids ate some of it, and I gave the extra away to the neighbors—just like my grandmother would have done. By the end of the week, my feelings were manageable. I had released my grief through spontaneous body work. It couldn't have worked out better even if I had planned it. For me, at that time, a spur-of-the-moment project that honored what my grandmother taught me was best.

A client, Sarah, lost her mother to cancer. Sarah worried that she hadn't taken good enough care of her mother because her mother died so suddenly. We talked about the cancer being spread in the lymph nodes before the doctors even detected it. Since it was in such an advanced stage, the prognosis for her mother's life was short. And because her mother was ninety years old, she opted for no treatment, so she didn't live long.

Even though Sarah knew all these things, she was still full of grief and guilt. She reported that the only time she felt relief was when she worked in her mother's rose garden. Her mother prized her roses above every-thing. Sarah said she could almost feel her mother there. I suggested that Sarah spend some time working the soil and using her creative visualization to have her mother with her.

Sarah came back to the next session feeling more peaceful. During the week, she spaded the entire rose garden, breaking up each dirt clump with her hands and visualizing her mother there. They had a good time together, discussing the funny things that happened in the family and telling each other how much they loved each other and missed being together. Now Sarah works in her garden several times a week—when-ever she needs to talk to her mother.

As you can see, each person must tailor their grief body work to fit their own situation. Find a way to keep your loved one in mind. For me, those dear ones are closer than you think.

Remember to keep yourself physically safe during your body work. And see that others are protected during this process also.

If you are grieving as a family, you may decide to include your chil-dren in your workouts. You could plant flowers or trees around your home or in the park. Many times, children like to participate in large-muscle activities as part of their grief process. Allow them to choose what they want to do. A soccer game in the park or a punching bag in the garage can be very therapeutic.

Get yourself involved with a therapist and consider their guidance if you wish. Only you can decide what's best for you.

Summary

The grieving process is varied and must be looked on as an individual path—like life itself. You can plan your grieving if you wish, but sometimes it just happens spontaneously, and that's great. Let it happen. Tailor your process to the things your loved one enjoyed. Follow your heart and it will lead you in the direction you should go.

Commitment

- Give yourself permission to grieve in your own way.
- Plan grieving according to the things you and your loved one enjoyed.
- Let your heart lead you.

PART 4

Getting Back
Into Daily Life

A Survivor: Abandoned, Abused, and Raped
Katy

I was born in a large metropolitan area and lived with my grandmother. My father was already married to another woman—not my mother. He had five children by his wife. After I was born, he abandoned both his wife and my mother.

My mother was busy with her own life, coming home once in a while to make sure my grandmother and I had food and the bills were paid. My mother was dating my half-brother's father, who was involved with the mafia. He also had a family at the time he dated my mother.

My mother worked as a waitress and, later, with the help of my half brother's father, became a house prostitute for the mafia in another city. That's why she wasn't around much.

However, when she did come home, everything revolved around her. She was the center of attention, and what she wanted mattered most. I never got much love from her.

I am grateful that my grandmother was around. She taught me to be resourceful. I had to do everything for myself, mainly because my grandmother was unable to get around the house. She weighed about three hundred pounds. I loved my grandmother. She was nurturing and kind and spent a lot of time with me. As I grew older, I was grateful she taught me to do things for myself, because my life was better for it.

When Mother came home from her out-of-town job, she stayed with us. There were times my mother and grandmother would argue, and I would hide in the bedroom. My brother's father left his wife and children and would also move into our house until my mother went back to work as a house prostitute.

My mother's sister, my Aunt Betty, came into my life when I was around seven years old. She lived in an apartment behind us. She married a man from Cleveland, Ohio, and moved away. Unfortunately, they couldn't have any children.

My grandma and I moved to Ohio and lived with Aunt Betty for about a year when I was seven and a half. My mother had just given birth to my brother, and Aunt Betty and her husband tried, unsuccessfully, to get custody of my brother, whom my mother abandoned to my grandmother just like she did me.

My grandmother died when I was about eleven. After her death, my mother boarded me out while she continued to work for the mafia out of town. During this time, I attended four or five different schools.

The first family she boarded me with didn't work out, so she found another family in the county where she was raised. While I was there, I was raped by a man who was a friend of the family I lived with.

I was pregnant and only twelve years old.

Child Protective Services (CPS) took me away from there and let me stay with Aunt Betty. CPS declared my mother an unfit parent. While I stayed with my aunt, I had to go to court, which was very scary. I testified about the rape. Later, I found out that the man who raped me went to jail.

My aunt took care of me until CPS placed me in a home for unwed mothers. I felt lonely and abandoned. I wanted to stay with Aunt Betty. I had the baby at age thirteen. After my baby boy was born, he was put up for adoption.

CPS put me and my little brother into the foster care system in separate homes until we each turned eighteen.

While I was in foster care, I realized that the only way to overcome all that I had experienced was to do well at school. So I put my energy into my studies and other school activities like music, swimming, baseball, and basketball.

I later married, but my husband abandoned me and our two sons when the youngest was only three weeks old and our older boy was two. This was so shocking to me, and all the abandonment I had experienced in my life came flooding back to me. How could he leave me with two small children?

I wasn't working at the time, and I had to go on welfare so I could raise my boys. But I was determined to fight to overcome the effects of my childhood and move on. I took care of my boys to the best of my ability.

I was on welfare for twelve years, but during that time, I devoted myself to my boys. I was involved in the PTA, Little League sports, and all the other activities my boys enjoyed. At the same time, I went back to school to get my bachelor's degree. I found a good job and have supported myself and my boys ever since.

My two boys grew into adulthood. One of them was killed by a hit-and-run driver at twenty-two years old. I was devastated. I felt like my world was falling to pieces. It felt like everyone was being taken from me again—just like when I was a child. I held on to my son's things long after his death. I didn't really want to believe he was gone.

I devoted myself to my work, stayed close to my church, and went to counseling. Somehow, I got through it.

My other son married and had four children. One was stillborn— another loss to deal with. I helped support my son and his family through his young adult years. I helped raise my grandkids just like my grandmother did for me. The children are grown now and living around the country. I visit them often.

I retired a few years ago and love to travel with friends and family. Spur-of-the-moment trips are great for me. I belong to a percussion group, work on my family history, and write poetry with the local poet laureate. I have had several of my works published.

I am in the process of publishing a workbook for abuse survivors. I want to share this resource with teenagers who are in that transition period of their lives and anyone else who is in need of this resource. I hope it will be of help to anyone who has had similar experiences in their lives.

Particularly through my writing and counseling, I've come to recognize the good things that were there, regardless of the awful parts of my life:

- I learned to rely on myself.
- Family is very important to me. I keep my family around me.
- Friends are like an extra family to me.
- Education is key to having a good life.
- I value friendships.
- Laughter is a key to survival.
- I find joy in the moment.
- It is healing to help others along the same path.

CHAPTER 20

Mistaken Childhood Beliefs and the Grieving Process

I have this strange feeling that I'm not myself anymore. It's hard to put into words, but I guess it's like I was fast asleep, and someone came, disassembled me, and hurriedly put me back together again. That sort of feeling.
—Haruki Murakami, *Sputnik Sweetheart*

Tragedy and the grief that follows are never easy to let go of. Sometimes, mistaken childhood beliefs get in the way of moving beyond the trauma. At times, they even keep us stuck in the past.

Good things and bad things happen during early childhood years that help form our outlook on life. If you were abused, abandoned, or neglected as a child, you might see the world as unsafe, according to the things that happened to you. For instance, my youthful view of the world was that men would abandon me (because my father died). I know now that all men won't abandon me, but I didn't know it then.

Sometimes, as we grow into adulthood, we come to understand our mistaken beliefs on an intellectual level, but emotionally, that little child inside us still harbors those ideas. These mistaken views may be conscious so we can talk about them or we may be unaware that they are present and coloring our outlook on the world.

As we look at our relationships and the motivations behind the people we choose to be with, including the circumstances that surround us, we can see that they are not unlike those we came from in childhood—unhelpful as they may be.

As you grow into adulthood, you may look for a relationship, thinking you'll get those childhood needs met, or you may connect with someone who reminds you of your suffering.

Think back on your early years and list several of the possible mistaken concepts you could have formed.

Outline the mistaken beliefs that you can think of.

When my father was killed, I firmly believed that men would not stay in my life. My father had left me, so that was the way the world worked. My childhood brain figured things out the best it could. Men would leave, and women had to take care of everything. With this view of life firmly entrenched in my head, but not in my conscious mind, I married just after college.

I (unknowingly) clung to my new husband in the beginning of our relationship. I didn't want him to leave like my father had. I did everything I could to keep my husband happy. If he wanted to buy something, we got it. We bought a television with some of the money my mother had saved for my education because he wanted it. (My mother was upset.) We did everything his way. I learned to cook the special foods he loved—lemon meringue pie, cinnamon rolls, and chili sauce. I didn't ask anything from him because I was afraid he would abandon me.

Mistaken belief: Men abandon the family.

It didn't take long for me to become resentful of this pattern. There was no reciprocity in our relationship. He had been raised by a single mother also, so neither of us knew any better. Slowly, I learned to share my feelings and talk through problems, asking for help when I needed it. Our partnership became more equal when I finally let go of my childhood issues enough to say, "I love you and want to be with you, but if you have another agenda, you may go." Of course, he stayed. The abandonment issue was mine, not his.

At that time, the balance of power in our relationship shifted to a more equal footing. We now have a better partnership than we did when we started out. But it's taken us a lot of hard work and years to change this pattern. We are fifty years into our marriage now, and life is good.

Louella came in for therapy because she couldn't get over the death of her husband. "I should be relieved," she said. "He flew into raging fits about once a week. He beat me often, blackening my eyes and at times breaking my ribs. I don't know why I stayed with him.

"He had a heart attack in the middle of one of his rages and died. I should be glad he's gone, but I'm depressed and lonely without him."

She continued, "Life is boring now because there are only nice people around. I guess I miss the excitement of the raging. I know that doesn't make any sense. No one should miss being beaten, but I do."

Louella grew up in a home where her father beat her mother and the children. Battery was a way of life for her.

Mistaken belief: Battery is part of my life.
Mistaken belief: Battery is exciting.
Mistaken belief: Kind people are boring.

Louella worked hard in therapy. She explored abusive childhood memories. She wrote and journaled. She created mantras and visualizations to build her self-esteem. She built a relationship with a wise internal mentor—a best friend who had passed away several years before. We explored the dynamics of an addiction to battery and pain. She slowly healed with therapy and the support of a caring group at her church. When I last saw her, she was happy and dating a quiet (boring) gentleman who volunteered at the local Big Brothers.

New belief: It still feels different to be around kind people, but I'm getting used to it.

Anna was raised by her grandmother in New York City. She had no idea who her father was, and her mother showed up about once a month to fight with her grandmother.

"I just hid in my room when my mother and grandmother fought," Anna said.

After high school, she attended college and married. At the birth of her second daughter, her husband abandoned the family. Anna raised the two girls on her own.

She came in for therapy several months after her older girl, Cecilia, was killed by a drunk driver who ran his car up onto the sidewalk, hitting her daughter and smashing down a street sign, a stop sign, and a lamp pole. Anna couldn't get past Cecilia's death.

"The only way I can force myself to go to work is to pretend Cecilia is away on vacation. I imagine she'll be home soon. I plan a homecoming party for her, and when it gets close to the date, I make an excuse for her to stay a little longer. I know my thinking isn't realistic. It's all in my head, but it keeps me going to work every day. I think I'm crazy, and I don't know how to get past all this."

We talked about Anna, the survivor. She functioned after the abandonment of her father and her mother. She'd finished high school and college. She'd dealt with her husband's leaving and held down a good job. She'd raised two beautiful children. Could she survive Cecilia's death? She was already doing it in her own way.

Mistaken belief: My family abandons me.

Anna had never looked at herself as strong; but as we talked about her life, she could see her resilience. Through creative visualization, she found her wise mentor—her grandmother. (No surprise there.) As Anna meditated daily, she found Cecilia and her grandmother together often.

Besides visualizations, Anna wrote to Cecilia, telling her how sad she was without her. Anna wished she could have protected Cecilia. Anna wanted Cecilia to have the happy life Anna never had.

Mistaken belief: I will never have a happy life. That's only for others.

Anna composed Cecilia's response in which Cecilia told her mother that she missed her also. She was glad they could spend time together when Anna meditated. Anna's grandmother and Cecilia encouraged Anna to surround herself with the family and loved ones who lived near her.

Anna had put all her hopes in both her daughters having happy lives and had forgotten about her own. Anna put together a list of things that she wanted to do in life. She enjoyed Native American music, so she spent time listening daily. She loved to write and put together a workbook to help others who had experienced the trauma she had been through.

Her younger daughter married, and Anna loved to care for the grandchildren that came along. She bought a house and fixed it up just as she wanted. She found daily peace in her meditation, writing, and being with her family.

The tragedy in our lives can bring us gifts as we face our mistaken childhood beliefs about life.

I learned some assertiveness skills and gained the ability to ask for what I wanted in my marriage.

New belief: Many families have a father and mother. Men don't always leave their families.

Louella let go of her belief that battery is a normal everyday occurrence.

New belief: Healthy relationships are okay. Kind people are not boring.

Anna filled her life with happiness and is now enjoying extended family who lives nearby and supports her.

New belief: Family doesn't always abandon you.

What are the gifts you have found through the trauma you have suffered? What are your new beliefs?

Summary

Tragedy and the emotions that follow it are difficult to release. Mistaken childhood beliefs can keep us stuck in past and present trauma. Look at your growing-up years. If there was abuse or misfortune during the past, has it colored your outlook on the difficult times you are experiencing today?

There are many tools to use to overcome mistaken beliefs: journaling, visualizations with a wise mentor, letter-writing, and mantras. Talk with a therapist or a trusted friend. Ask for feedback concerning the parts of your life that aren't working right now. Find support in healthy relationships in your community and family. Recognize the childhood messages that you have changed and look for those that are keeping you stuck in negative patterns.

As you explore your mistaken beliefs and work through past trauma, you will be able to relate to the world in a healthier way and rewrite your mistaken ideas.

Commitment

- List possible mistaken childhood beliefs.
- How do they influence you today?
- Use your creative visualizations to heal mistaken beliefs.
- Write letters to your loved ones.
- Focus on your strengths.
- Use other healing techniques to create your best self.

CHAPTER 21

Biography

Whether I shall turn out to be the hero of my own life, or whether that station will be held by anybody else, these pages must show.
—Charles Dickens, *David Copperfield*

Creating a biography of a loved one who has passed on will become a memorial that will allow your loved one to live on in the hearts and minds of those left behind. Think about writing their life story, including trials and triumphs, struggles and successes, and the effort they expended to find their way through life. You never know when another family member may have to walk that same road. This will be a time for you to explore their outlook on living—their personal philosophy, if you will.

Researchers at Emory University in the mid-1990s found that kids who knew their family stories were much more resilient when tragedy struck. Children who knew where they came from were able to bounce back from problems easier than those who didn't. So write your family stories for your kids. Write biographies of your family members. It's one of the greatest gifts you can give your children and yourself. You might find that your own resilience is bolstered.

Writing can be the means of keeping you out of depression, and it enables you to express your sadness. Journaling then becomes a form of grief therapy—a way to move beyond the death. But it can also be a way to bind your loved one to you and others who live on.

"But I don't like to write."

"I don't know where to start."

"What would I write about?"

Writing isn't the only way. Interview family members or create a story video of your loved one.

Following are some ideas to get past these obstacles.

Biography, Video, or Interview as a Memorial

Put a picture in your mind of your loved one who has passed away. Ask the following questions of loved ones as part of your interview. Video yourself answering these questions. Let these questions be a jumping-off point for everyone to share stories and memories.

What do people tell you about them?

How do others say you are like your loved one?

"You look so much like your mother."

"Your hands are just like your father's."

"You have the same mannerisms as your uncle."

These statements draw us close to our departed family, but they also give us bittersweet moments of sadness as we think of them and grieve.

What are some of the defining characteristics of your loved one?

A way of walking?

A droll sense of humor?

A balding head?

Weatherworn hands?

Choose something about your deceased family member that draws you to them. Let this significant feature help you begin your biography. From that personality feature or physical trait, list the specific memories that relate to that characteristic. Now begin to write from your recollections.

Jess wrote about his grandfather after he died as part of his grieving process.

Jess loved the seashore just like his grandfather and spent hours walking the sand like he'd done with his grandfather. His hands looked like his grandfather's.

> My grandfather—we called him Papa—was raised on an island off the coast of Maine. He loved the seashore. I remember, as a child, digging for clams with him. Early in the morning we would hop in Papa's small rowboat and motor around the island to a secluded spot. Papa always wore his old rubber boots, but I loved to roll my pants up and go barefoot. I can still remember the squishy feeling of mud through my toes and the sucking sound when I pulled my feet out of the mud. Papa handed me a hoe with a short handle and only four small tines on it to dig with. He took one just like it in his weathered hands and began to dig in the sand. I remember watching the muscles in his hands work the soil, looking for clams. I wanted my hands to be big and strong like his.

> He gave me a roller (basket) of my own and told me if I got it full to the top, he'd buy me a pop at the little store in town on the way home. I dug and slurped the clams out of the muddy water. He always said I was doing good when I got the bottom of the basket covered. By then, my back was tired of bending so I knelt down on my hands and knees and really got muddy.

> After a while I stopped to build a sandcastle or look for sea shells, and Papa would remind me about the soda. Then I would start again. He told me stories about fishing on his dad's boat when he was a boy.

Jess had been a caregiver for Papa. It was hard for him to let go. The journaling helped. He and his family recorded stories about Papa for future generations.

Especially if you have been the caregiver, writing about this suffering and death can summarize the ultimate service you gave—that of creating a loving environment for one to pass from this life to the next. The legacy of your kindness can live for generations in your family.

You get the idea. Create a biographical memorial for your loved one. Be sure to keep your tone realistic. It's difficult if you memorialize this person into sainthood so that no one identifies with him or her. Keep it human.

Take an additional step and write your own memory of the loss of your family member. Many times, this will include the time you spent caring for your dying loved one—watching them suffer and fade away.

For some, writing is easier than talking. It is a solitary expression when speech is not private enough.

Whatever your family story is, record it for future generations.

Summary

Writing a biography of your loved one can be a means of keeping their memory alive for generations to come. Choose a defining characteristic to begin your writing. Journaling your own role in the death and suffering of a family member can be a lasting legacy of love for those who follow you. Kids are more resilient if they know their family stories. Give them the gift of knowing where they came from.

Commitment

- Create a lasting legacy of love.
- Compose a biography about your loved one.
- Choose a defining characteristic and begin there.
- Journal your role in the death of your loved one.

CHAPTER 22

A Memorial Tribute

*Silently, one by one, in the infinite meadows
of heaven,
Blossomed the lovely stars, the forget-me-nots
of the angels.*
—Henry Wadsworth Longfellow,
"Evangeline: A Tale of Acadie"

When we lose a loved one, part of the grieving process is remembering the wonderful relationship we had with them. Our children enjoy talking about the fun they had with their grandmother, who died recently at age ninety-four. They include happy times, funny times, difficult times, and sad times. This grandmother will live on as part of their lives forever.

Sometimes after the death of a cherished family member, the hurt is too great to memorialize them right away. The grief is too new. After my father's death, my mother put away everything that reminded her of him. It was just too hard for her to be in touch with her feelings at first. She had to live with her loss for a few years before we could talk about him and look at the things that had belonged to him—

like his old Army trunks full of memorabilia and the things he had collected from his travels.

Give yourself permission to be at the place that is best for you right now. If you are ready to create a place of honor, good; but if not, give yourself a break and wait until you are ready. Your heart will let you know what is best for you.

Here are some questions for you to consider in making this decision:

- What is my relationship with the deceased?
- Am I preoccupied with the death event? Explain.
- Do I avoid recollections right now? If so why?
- Am I able to organize my memories at this time?
- Am I comfortable creating a memorial? What kind would be best?
- How do I want to continue with life in relationship to the deceased?
- What is my relationship with my living family right now?

_____

_____

_____

_____

_____

Creating a memorial can include the likes and hobbies of the deceased. If your grandmother stitched a beautiful quilt, hang it in a place of honor. Sometimes after creating a memorial for someone, it's easier to accept their death and move on. Take care of yourself and those who are still living by creating a compilation of family memories.

Here are some ideas:

- Light a candle at church or in a memorial corner at home.
- Take flowers or other tributes to the grave. (Our children took pinecones to my mother's grave because she had a large pine tree at home. We were always picking up pinecones.)
- Plant a tree in their memory.
- Plant a garden in their name. Our grandson just finished an Eagle Scout project for a widow who had donated a garden to the city in honor of her husband, who recently passed away.

- Create a service project in their honor.
- Create a scholarship fund in the deceased's name.
- A friend whose daughter was killed by a drunk driver became very involved in Mothers Against Drunk Driving as a tribute to her daughter's memory.
- Share stories of your loved one.
- Keep a memory journal of happy times.
- Write them a letter.
- Write a poem about them.
- Have a reminiscing party and collect favorite recollections from everyone in attendance. Put them all in a scrapbook.
- Create a memory scrapbook of pictures and stories. Make copies for everyone in the family.
- Sew a memory quilt.
- Hang a collage of old photographs on the wall.
- Design memes as a tribute to them.
- Have a bubble memorial. A client and her family met at the cemetery after the death of her infant daughter, gave everyone a bottle of soapy liquid, and everyone sent bubbles with angel-wishes skyward in her honor. After at a family party, everyone wrote their wishes down for the family to keep in a special book.
- Arrange a table where you can display pictures and hobbies of your loved one.
- Picture your loved one walking beside you when you're feeling alone. Talk to them and listen to their advice.
- Spend time with your deceased family member or friend in your daily meditations if you like.

Scientific American reports that many rituals we perform daily make a lot of sense and can be effective.

Helen grieved the loss of her son. She left his toothbrush in the bathroom for several years after his death. Each night before bed, she took it out of its holder and thought of him before she brushed her own teeth. She said it gave her comfort to remember he had been part of her life. That small act helped her remember him.

After Rulon's grandmother died, his children wanted to put pinecones on her grave. Rulon thought this was crazy. It would make her headstone look messy. The kids had picked up the pinecones from Grandmother's yard each Saturday before Rulon mowed the lawn. They wanted Grand-mother to know they remembered her and helping with her pinecones.

Summary

While the memory of your loved one is still fresh, it may be too early to create a memorial. After you are better acquainted with your grief, create the kind of memorial that will allow your loved one to live on in the hearts of family and friends. Let your memories decide how, when—and even if—you will create a place of honor for your loved one.

Commitment

- Sit with your grief until you are ready to build a memorial.
- Let your heart help you decide when and what to create.
- Create your memorial.
- Share it with family and friends.

CHAPTER 2 3

Positive Thinking

Sometimes it takes a heartbreak to shake us awake and help us see we are worth so much more than we're settling for.
—Mandy Hale, *The Single Woman*

We all react to trauma in different ways, depending on our background and emotional makeup. If you are already predisposed to negative thinking, the disaster you have just experienced may make your negative self-talk even more pronounced.

Looking at your reactions to the trauma in your life in a negative way can make your symptoms worse. This type of thinking can heighten your anxiety and depression.

Research at the University of Oregon has shown that those who have experienced trauma and have negative thinking patterns will be more likely to feel shame when given negative feedback.

Take a "before the trauma" inventory and see where you stood:
On a scale from 1 to 5, with 5 being the most positive:
Before the trauma:

_____ I was happy with my life before the trauma.

_____ I had positive self-talk.

_____ I liked myself.

_____ I was anxious about many things.

_____ I found pleasure throughout my day.

_____ I liked to look for the beauties surrounding me and take joy in them.

_____ I loved being around people.

_____ I found good in everyone.

If your score is below 12, you probably have a predisposition for negative thinking patterns.

If this is the case, exposure to trauma can be a wake-up call—a great gift, if you will—to suggest that you look at your thinking patterns. Take stock and see where you need to improve.

Joe had grown up in a home with lots of negativity and arguing. He always watched for the worst to happen in all he did—even before the accident: a car didn't see Joe's motorcycle and sideswiped him, sending him to the hospital with a broken leg and fractured elbow. His leg healed, but his arm was slow to recover.

Joe came into counseling with a goal to let go of the trauma from the accident. He was sure all his depression came from that event. As he began to focus on his thought patterns, he could see that he had been a negative thinker his whole life. He would come up with the worst thing that could possibly happen in any given situation. We jokingly began to call it "disaster thinking."

Joe was an expert at disaster thinking. For instance, he was called in to meet with the boss at work. He telephoned for an emergency therapy session. He was sure he was going to get fired. During the entire session, he gave reasons he was going to be let go.

The next day, he met with the boss who gave him a commendation for his work and asked him to train some new employees in their division. He called me after the meeting—excited and a little embarrassed over his fear. The incident was a great opportunity for Joe to look at his negative thinking patterns and begin to establish some positive ones.

Joe and I discussed the concept of mindfulness. He sat in the office, aware of his breathing, as he inhaled to the count of four, held to the count of four, and exhaled to the count of eight. He noticed the white armchair he sat in, his feet resting on the floor, his elbow (still in a sling) resting comfortably on the padded arm of the chair.

We talked about internal mindfulness—being aware of feelings for the moment.

"I want a feeling of happiness," he said. "I spend every Saturday afternoon with my four- and six-year-old kids at the park. They love life. I want to experience that joy, but how do I go about getting it?"

Joe shifted in his chair. "When I watch my kids, they are in a state of happiness. I know they have good thoughts at that moment, but the happiness goes even further. It seems to fill their whole body. That's what I want."

He proposed filling himself with feelings—not just thoughts. We talked about joyfulness as a state of being, not just a thought.

Joe wanted not only to eradicate his negative thinking but he also wanted a positive full body experience. He set a goal to feel joyful three times each day. He began a feelings-thoughts log, calling it a "Beyond Positive Thinking Journal."

We have many experiences each day. If we are tuned to look for the negative, we'll find it. If we use our mindfulness to be aware of our total experience, we can find the good in it. Remember, mindfulness includes being curious about every part of your moment.

Let's look at some of Rick Hanson's suggestions in *Hardwiring Happiness*. The more you infuse yourself with positive experiences, the greater happiness you'll feel.

1. Be aware of your breathing and begin your breathing exercise.
2. Notice the positive in your experience—something enjoyable about your immediate moment.
3. Remember a positive moment in your life and think of something in the here and now or in the past that you are happy about.
4. Be mindful of someone you enjoy. Remember a positive relationship with someone you like.
5. Think of the goodness in you. Reflect on things that give you strong, happy, and loving feelings.
6. Be grateful and give thankfulness for your surroundings.

Spend some time with each exercise. Let them come to the forefront of your awareness. Feel the positive. This practice will begin to infuse you with positive energy.

Joe began to practice this process and found himself in a happier place than he had been before the accident.

Here are a few of his reflections of "happiness" moments that he journaled:

- Cheering with the crowd at a Red Sox game/feeling the power of collective human experience.
- Warm water washing over my body in the shower/being renewed and feeling clean.
- Sitting in the warm sunshine to eat my lunch/allowing healing energy to fill my soul and feeling pampered.
- Hearing that a coworker's cancer test came back negative/bursting with tears and being full of gratitude.
- Watching the crocus leaves push up through the ground with my kids/borrowing their wonder at the beauty of nature and feeling it myself.

Set a goal for yourself to walk beyond negativity even though tragedy is present in your life. Fill your being with joy.

Take some time to write some happiness moments either in this book or in your personal journal. Record one every night before bed or in the morning before you begin your day. Then take the post-tragedy survey (see chapter 1) after a week and again after a month to see if you have changed your thinking patterns.

_____

_____

_____

_____

I don't think of all the misery, but
of the beauty that still remains.
—Anne Frank

Summary

Tragedy distresses everyone differently. If you are disposed to negative thinking already, it can add to your anxiety and depression that may come from the trauma. Look at your thinking patterns to see where you are on the negative-thinking scale.

Begin to turn your thought patterns around by using your mindfulness meditation to see the good everywhere. Remember good times and people that you enjoy being with. Express gratitude.

Commitment

- Assess your negative thinking.
- Use your mindfulness to find the good around you.
- Meditate daily on the positives in your life.
- Remember happy moments.
- Experience gratitude each day.

CHAPTER 24

Personal Mantras

The Mirror Prayer
I see you man in the mirror. I see you and raise you. I will be better today than you were yesterday, and tomorrow you will be better than I was today.

—Dimitri Zaik, *Ink Bleeder*

I like the quote introducing this chapter, because it's a new start for the beginning of each day.

Mantras are repeated phrases or messages of truth. Because our minds can run off in every direction at once like an wild horse, it is necessary to bridle them. Mine still runs off sometimes, but I can gently bring it back into focus with a mantra.

I find peace with my mindful moments and my mantras.

If we have experienced a trauma, we can get stuck in the anxiety, fear, and grief of the moment. When I mourn, I remember to go into my feelings, feel my sorrows, and then get out of them. Mantras are one of the ways I do that—to center myself again to let in the love and light around me.

How will these short sayings change our feelings about the disaster that we've just experienced? Thinking creates feelings. If I repeat or chant my mantras, my thinking focuses on them and my feelings begin to lift out of my anxiety and depression—not all at once, but over time. And the benefit that comes from doing this is that I have improved my quality of life because I now find joy and peace in my life where I may not have even noticed it before.

Like everything else in this book, I want to offer the general principle and allow you to do the work of creating your own recovery process. As you read this chapter, I want to challenge you to invent mantras that will heal the specific holes in your heart. I can tell you my mantras, but because our tragedies have been different, we have different issues and different solutions.

Deciding which direction you want your mind to go is a personal goal. Therefore, creating your own mantras is important if you want to walk in the direction of your life values. Ask your wise mentor to help you. The wisdom is within you. Tap into it.

What is your relationship with your grief?

What is your direction?

Where do you want to end up?

How Do You Write Mantras?

Once you have an idea of where you want to go with your grieving process, you can begin to write your mantras. Look at the parts of your life that you would like to change. What are your goals? Sit with your negative energy. It is part of you. Acknowledge it and decide how you can attract peace and love to your life.

- List the parts of you that need to heal.
- Write them in the order of importance.
- Begin with the first one.
- Be in the moment with it.
- Ask your wise mentor what action you need to take.
- Compose several positive statements.
- Revise them as you wish.
- Choose the positive statement you like best.

That's your new mantra.

My father was killed when I was young. I felt my best friend had been snatched from me. Life had been ripped away. I was unlovable. So I have mantras like these:

- My father loves me and is there for me.
- I am loveable.
- What I am—the positive and the negative—is enough.
- My life is abundant.

At times, you may run across quotes or statements that speak to you. Use them as mantras if you wish. We all gravitate to themes of light, love, peace, and joy. Find the phrases and images that tug at your heart. For instance:

- Light is stronger than dark.
- Love chases away hate.
- Today, I will live in an attitude of peace.
- I will see life through the eyes of joy.

The other places I glean mantras from are wise spiritual leaders, authors, and ancient scripture:

1. "Memory is more indelible than ink."—Anita Loos, *Kiss Hollywood Good-Bye*
2. "Mistakes are the portals of discovery."—James Joyce, *The Book of Blessings*
3. "The greatest of these is charity."—I Cor. 13:13 (KJV)
4. "So long as we love, we serve."—Robert Louis Stevenson, *Lay Morals*
5. "A man with outward courage dares to die; a man with inner courage dares to live."—Lao Tzu, *Tao Te Ching*

Here is a mantra about fear that a friend of mine uses:

I must not fear. Fear is the mind-killer. Fear is the little-death that brings total obliteration. I will face my fear. I will permit it to pass over me and through me. And when it has gone past I will turn the inner eye to see its path. Where the fear has gone there will be nothing. Only I will remain.

—Frank Herbert, *Dune*

As you begin the process of speaking to your own soul, follow these five points:

1. Take some time to look at yourself.
2. Find the emptiness in your being.
3. Ask yourself, "Where am I in my healing process?"
4. Identify your greatest needs.
5. Discover what deficits you find in your life from personal tragedy.

Now, look at the successes you have had in your life with the following five points:

1. What gives you great joy?
2. What have you accomplished in life?
3. How did you add light to the world today?
4. List the beauties of nature that give you pleasure.
5. What life lessons have you learned from your personal tragedy?

Each of these can shape and change your mantras. Include them as part of your meditation. This is a journey of change that will happen over time—not something to be fixed in the moment. As you and your wise mentor discuss your healing process, rewrite and modify your self-talk as is best for you. Follow your internal guide and listen to your own wisdom. Healing is within you. It always has been.

Writing in a journal is a good place to start this process. Keep the intellectual and pull in the emotional aspect of it. I matured through my personal tragedy. I would not have the insight and love for others and their difficulties that I do today if I hadn't suffered myself. Look not only at your deficits but also at the strength you have because of your trials.

Use the mantras and memes you design in your creative visualization. Turn them into mini movies if you like. Your path to healing can be one of joy and self-discovery. Take time to bless your own life, and in doing so, you will bless the lives of others.

Summary

Because our minds can become scattered at times—especially in times of grief and loss—it's important to have some mantras that you say daily to keep light, love, and peace in your life. Create your own mantras for the greatest healing effect. Ask your wise mentor to help you. Choose the issues you want to work on. Order them. Write positive statements about each, and say them daily.

You can also find positive statements that you read elsewhere to include in your daily meditation if you wish. Surround yourself with peace and light to mend the sadness in your heart.

Commitment

- Read your journal to help you focus on your healing path.
- Decide the issues you want to heal.
- Write positive statements about each with the help of your internal mentor.
- Use them daily in your meditation.

CHAPTER 25

Friends

In times of grief and sorrow, I will hold you
and rock you and take your grief and make it
my own. When you cry, I cry, and when you
hurt, I hurt. And together we will try to hold
back the floods of tears and despair and make
it through the potholed street of life.
—Nicholas Sparks, *The Notebook*

Over the years, it has been very helpful for me to have trusted friends
to share my grief. Different trials have surfaced in my life from time to
time, and it is as if I have been provided with angels of mercy to help
me process whatever difficulty I'm going through.

A friend and I walked each evening while I cared for my mother,
who was dying of cancer. I needed a little time every night to get some
exercise and to share my sadness. She gave me both. Another friend and
I had lunch together when we were both going through problems with
our teenage children. Another friend took me to local university lectures
when I felt life closing in on me. Whether it was a friend, another young

mother, a coworker, a teacher, or my spouse, I was grateful for those relationships. They all meant the world to me.

How do you find good friends? Have you ever been burned in friendship?

How can you know if someone is safe to talk to? I've seen clients struggle with friends who may give tons of advice to do things their way, not the clients'. I've also seen the heartache caused when a confidante tells all their friends what you've said in private, betraying a trust. I've witnessed the dynamic between friends where one might spend the entire time they're together talking about their own problems and not letting the other get a word in edgewise.

Watch out for negative talkers, those who like violent activities, those who are mean to animals, people who love to push others around, and people who like to tell victim stories. If you find these characteristics in a person, think twice about the relationship. If your situation is such that you are unable to separate yourself from those people (for instance, a family member), be cautious about sharing the details of your life with them. There are lots of kind people in the world. Look for those individuals to be your friends.

Here are some of the traits I recommend you look for in a safe person to trust your deepest feelings with:

- **Someone who listens.** Find a friend who will listen to you as you share your heartfelt grief. You don't need any advice at a time like this—just the experience of connecting with someone on a feeling level will be enough. It is very validating to have another human being hear your fear, pain, sadness, and other discomforting feelings.

- **Someone who will mirror what you say.** Having a friend that can reflect the things you have to say without judging you or your situation will feel liberating. All they need to say is, "I hear you." You can ask your friend for this gift to make sure he or she responds as you would like. We all come with backgrounds and baggage—opinions of how things "should" be. But your friend can suspend judgment at a time like this and offer no advice.

- **Someone who will mourn with you.** Change is part of life. It is inevitable. It's the only constant we experience. For me, grief and change go hand in hand. I may be enthusiastic about whatever new is coming into my life, but I will always grieve for what is past. It is authenticating to have someone you can mourn the past with. Dying is part of life. It will touch us all. For me to have a friend who will lament my loss with me is one of the greatest gifts I can experience.

- **Someone you are grateful for.** I am profoundly grateful for those people in my life who have shared in my grieving process. What a precious offering this is! As I unburden myself of fear and sadness, those feelings melt away because of the emotional connection with and validation of my friend.
- **Someone who loves the same activities you do.** Loss is difficult, and it's good to go into your feelings and then get out of them. It's a great release to go do something fun with a friend. It's important to have a good time. Grieving and letting go can happen in so many ways, as we've discussed in other chapters. Invite a friend and listen to music you like, go dancing, see a concert, go to an art gallery or museum—whatever you love. Start to enjoy life again with a friend.
- **Someone who can help in times of need.** A friend of mine lost her husband. She didn't know how to set the timer on the automatic sprinklers or start the snowblower. Another friend needed help sorting out her husband's estate. A neighbor who was a lawyer came to her aid. Surround yourself with friends and neighbors who can help fill out your knowledge if need be.

This kind of emotional connection not only happens with friends—I had the privilege of working with clients in this capacity every day. I never finished a therapy session without experiencing a deep sense of gratitude for the emotional connection that I was fortunate enough to participate in.

A therapist is a person you can develop a caring relationship with, but it is a temporary connection that you will let go of as soon as you have the insights and skills needed to continue life's journey on your own. A friendship can be a relationship you enjoy for a lifetime. A therapist has been trained to look for family-system patterns along with behavior dysfunction to help the client identify the changes they want to make in their lives. A friend can give wonderful support and positive advice, but they don't have the training to help a person identify life patterns they desire to modify.

Find a good therapist if you like. A professional can assist in the process and give you the support you need in your time of sorrow.

Summary

Friends are important as we grieve our loss. Find friends that listen, mirror what you say, mourn with you, love to do the same things you do, and can help in times of need. You will feel that emotional connection and enjoy the safety of love as you grieve your loss.

Commitment

- Look at the people you are associated with.
- Are they safe?
- Find those who will support you.
- Share your grief.

CHAPTER 26

Creating Joy in Your Life after Tragedy

I have heard there are troubles of more than
*   one kind.*
Some come from ahead and some come from
*   behind.*
But I've bought a big bat. I'm all ready you
*   see.*
Now my troubles are going to have troubles
*   with me!*
—Dr. Seuss, *I Had Trouble in Getting to Solla Sollew*

Joy dissolves fear.
Joy heals grief.
Joy dissipates darkness.
Joy brings light into our lives.
Light is always stronger than dark.
Joy is the absence of shame.
    When tragedy strikes, survivor guilt can set in, causing shame. Shameful thought processes often block out recognition of positive things or our

sense of worthiness to feel joy. Our thoughts can go something like this:

- Maybe I could have prevented the accident if only I had . . .
- Maybe I had a disagreement with my loved one that morning, and I'm sorry. If only I had . . .
- I could have suggested . . . and maybe the accident wouldn't have happened. If only I had . . .
- If I had only taken better care of my loved one, they wouldn't have died.
- It should have been me instead of them.

The negative statements we can make about ourselves are limitless. How do we eradicate our shame and find joy?

I could ask that question to a hundred people and get a hundred distinctive answers. We are all unique. We find joy in our own ways.

Happiness is not something ready-made. It comes from your own actions.

—Dalai Lama

I like the preceding quote because it jars me out of my "stinking thinking" when I'm in a negative mind-set. I know that my thinking creates my feelings. So I lighten up on myself and work on letting go of my guilt.

One of the first things I do is pay attention to mindful moments of joy. It is autumn as I am writing this—almost down to freezing at night—but my tomatoes are still ripening on the vine. They don't get quite as sweet as they do in the summer sun, but they struggle valiantly to become pale pink and then a deeper red. I find joy in watching this process. Ripening isn't as easy as it was in the summer, but it's happening.

When I've suffered a tragedy and I am filled with grief, I have to work a little harder to find moments of joy in my life, but I can still find them. Like the tomatoes, I have to be a little more valiant than at other times.

It's a good time to look at my feelings and ask myself some open-ended questions (questions that can't be answered with a yes or no).

- What do I have to do to fill myself with love?
- What will bring joy back into my life?
- What do I have to do to let go of my negative thinking?

Visit with your wise mentor and create an action list.

Now, this doesn't mean that you just abandon your grief and go forward with a happily-ever-after life. We all need time to go into our feelings of grief, but then, we need to get out of them for a time and rest. And we can repeat the process. Look for the new gifts that have come into your life from this tragedy.

Sue Ann felt bitter about her life. Her husband was killed in Afghanistan. She couldn't get out of her anger at being alone in life.

A friend, Lela, often sat with Sue Ann and witnessed her struggles. "Look for the good around you," she advised.

"There isn't any good around me," Sue Ann retorted.

"You have two beautiful children, a warm house, and a way to support yourself."

"True," Sue Ann said. "I guess I do."

A gentle breeze lifted Sue Ann's hair.

"Be grateful for the breeze," Lela said. "Find joy in the moment."

"I can't find joy in any moment just yet." Sue Ann looked at her friend, who was such a support through her greatest struggles. "But I can be grateful for this moment. It will help me let go of my anger. I can work toward joy, but I'm not there now."

"Understandable," Lela said. "Jot down some things that will help you reach this goal."

Sue Ann began her journey out of anger and toward joy.

It's important that we look inward to find the things that bring joy to our lives. Our place of pleasure may come from similarities to our family and friends. But it could also come from individual things different from those around us.

Remember, thinking is habitual. The more time you spend with your mindful moments and your meditation, the more joy you will find in life.

I make a conscious effort to bring light and love into my being. Mindful breathing, a positive view of my surroundings, a feeling of joy, and allowing the light of the day or the comfort of the darkness to penetrate my soul brings me to a good place. The important thing is to surround myself with light and love.

Here are some suggestions of activities that might bring you pleasure:
- Listen to uplifting music
- Exercise
- Practice yoga
- Walk with a friend

- Read just for fun
- Listen to a friend
- Go to lunch with a buddy
- Hug your neighbor
- Hug your family
- Enjoy someone else's happy moment
- Be grateful
- Expand your talents
- Journal
- Meditate
- Pray to connect with your higher power.

Finding joy will look different to each of us. I have an artist friend who finds joy in her paintings. If I were to paint for an hour a day, all I would find is frustration. However, if I write, I find happiness. I also delight in all children—especially my grandchildren. Spending time with them brings me joy.

Celebrate life in your own way. Allow joy to be your companion. Joy is a great friend.

Summary

After a death or a traumatic experience, guilt may engulf and even squelch our grief, leaving us stuck in a state of shock and the inability to move beyond the tragedy. If this happens to you, get out of your negative thinking and look for the good around you. Practice your mindful moments, look for positives in your life, and ask your wise mentor what you need to do to find your joy. Brainstorm ways you can find joy in your life.

Commitment

- Be mindful each day.
- Find the positives with those around you.
- Be grateful.
- Create a bucket list.
- Fill it.

CHAPTER 27

Making It Through the Holidays

Being a widow means being lonely in a room full of people, even family. [It means] wanting to tell him something important and then realizing that he probably knew before I did.

—Lynne

Holidays are a great time to enjoy family and friends. People look forward to being together. But it can also be a time of stress: making sure all the party foods are purchased and prepared, all the gifts are wrapped, and the travel arrangements have been made. Many people can easily feel overwhelmed by these tasks, especially when they are also dealing with the loss of loved one, sending those who survive into depression and isolation.

Many times, a loved one may become ill or pass away during a holiday, so each time that holiday comes back around, we are reminded of our loss.

Lynne and her husband of fifty-seven years learned he had terminal cancer several days before Thanksgiving. Holiday time was difficult that year. There were many goodbyes to be said and messages of love to convey. Lynne's husband passed away a few months later.

Here are her own words about life and the holidays:

> Being a widow means being lonely in a room full of people, even family. You never get over it and it doesn't get easier, but you do learn how to live in a new reality.
>
> I don't decorate the house for holidays now like I used to, and I try not to get melancholy. I don't play a lot of Christmas music. I mostly become robotic and go through the holiday preparations without thinking too deeply. I'm always happy to see the new year.

Finding a new way to celebrate the holidays can be a challenge. Each person must face this problem and find their own solution.

Samantha's husband was killed by a drunk driver just before Christmas. The couple had three children, ages ten, eight, and four.

"What was I to do?" Samantha asked. "I couldn't just cancel Christmas."

The family got through that first holiday with friends and family helping with the funeral and burial.

The next Christmas, Samantha and her children met her sister and family at a ski resort. "I just couldn't stay home," she said. "The cousins had a great time together, and it was a great distraction for me."

The year after that, they traveled to see an aunt who lived in Nova Scotia.

The following year, Samantha came in for some counseling.

"I'm running out of ideas for the holidays," Samantha said. "We have to stay home sometime."

"What would happen if you and the children planned some new traditions in your family?" I asked. "Include everyone's ideas."

The family brainstormed possible rituals and came up with a plan. They decided to prepare a mini celebration from each of the countries of origin for Samantha's and her husband's families. The kids had a great time researching possible new recipes to prepare and decorations to make. They checked out travel shows from the various countries and took virtual tours of the big city museums. They learned songs from each country and performed them on Christmas Eve for their grandparents.

Though their first Christmas at home wasn't easy without husband and father, incorporating new traditions helped each of the family members invite joy in and honor the memory of their loved one.

If you and your family have lost a loved one, like Samantha, plan some new traditions for yourselves. Make a new start. Include the children. They are full of unique ideas.

Here are a few ideas from clients that lost loved ones:

- Include an empty chair for your loved one who has passed away. Prepare some of their favorite dishes as part of your celebration.
- Have the children create an art collage of their favorite holiday memories of the past, including memories of the deceased.
- Make a special holiday scrapbook with specific stories of your loved one.
- Include embarrassing, funny, or spiritual moments.
- Tell stories about the courage and strength of those who have passed away.
- Research and write your great-grandparents' stories. Include thoughts of them being together with your loved one. Where are they all? Are they celebrating in heaven? If so, how?

Use this list as a jumping-off place to get your own creative juices flowing. You'll come up with great ideas that will fit your own family.

Ask your family to list several activities.

Happy holidays!

Summary

Holidays are times for loved ones and families to be together. These experiences can accentuate feelings of loss and grief. Take some time as a family to brainstorm activities that family and friends can do to celebrate those who have passed on and those who are together now. Include children in this task. They have great ideas. Life brings change, and change can bring loss. But if we focus on continuing to bring in joy, the loss is softened in light of the love you shared.

Commitment

- Call your family together for a meeting and plan your holiday time.
- Include memories of your loved one rather than running from them.
- Write stories about them.
- Include their favorite foods and activities.
- Use your mindful moments to cope with the loss.

PART 5

Final Touches for Becoming Your Best

A Family of Deaths
Theron

After my father's suicide, my mother's death from a long illness, and my brother's death in a house fire, I had to decide if I really believed in life after death.

The first death was that of my father. The whole thing was horrible. Just horrible.

I was at college. One morning before school, my pastor came to talk to me. I felt kind of confused, wondering why he had come to see me on a school day. It was weird. I had a sinking feeling in the pit of my stomach. Something was wrong, and I was nervous.

My father had been depressed for a long time. He went to a psychiatrist and got a prescription for an antidepressant. I think the medication made him worse instead of better. Not long after he began taking the pills, he took a gun and shot himself. I don't think he was in his right mind. I really don't.

The pastor told me that my father had shot himself. I was shocked at first—like it wasn't real. I had no idea this was coming. I sat down on the couch to try to get a grip. I felt myself shaking, and I began to cry.

Then, a totally weird thought popped into my head: *Well, Christmas is ruined.* I still remember thinking it. It was so random, and it didn't have anything to do with anything. It was such an odd thought. But it was December—December 12.

I sat for a few minutes and then knew I had to call my mother. She would be completely falling to pieces.

The whole thing seemed surreal. It was almost like it didn't really happen, because we had a closed-casket funeral. It was like he just went away. And in some ways, I think that was better for me. After his death, that's how I looked at it. He was just gone.

Right after the pastor left, I called my mother, and she was almost inconsolable. So my first thought was, *I need to get home.* The pastor said he would help me. I already had a plane ticket for the Christmas holidays, and I needed to get it changed. I wasn't in any shape to do it myself.

On the way home on the plane, I went from grieving myself to knowing that I would have to take care of my mother. And I had to get myself together pretty quickly because she needed me. I was the only one in the family who had any kind of faith, and she was really leaning on that. I had to put my feelings away so she had someone to rely on.

That's been my role in the family. I'm the one they all trust.

I put away my feelings and comforted my mother. The funeral took place, and the house seemed empty. My mother didn't know what to do, so she fed the raccoons in the backyard and went back to work as a checker at the grocery store.

I didn't really know if I should go back to college in January because I would be leaving Mom to fend for herself. My brother was there, but he was no support. But Mom wanted me to get my education, so I went back.

The next year, I changed schools. I went from a small two-year college to a larger university. I had several close friends. We enjoyed one another's company. I met a wonderful girl, fell in love, and married. Life went on, but I still had an empty place inside me. I still hadn't really grieved the loss of my father.

My wife and I have talked a lot about my grieving process. I didn't necessarily grieve right after my father died, but it happened a little bit at a time. Something would trigger it. My wife would be depressed, and I would freak out. Then we would talk about it, and I would calm down. At that time, I could see the connection with my father and his depression.

I read *The Loss That Is Forever* by Maxine Harris. I got a lot of insight from reading that. My grieving was a gradual process—a little bit here and a little bit there.

I finished my bachelor's and master's degrees. I found a job near my mother to be close to her.

A few years later, my mother got sick. She had been ill off and on through the winter and spring. We would take her to the hospital, and she would get better. Since she had been in and out of the hospital, we were somewhat prepared when she died—as prepared as you can be for death.

Even though I was pretty well settled over my father's passing, it seemed like I had to start all over with my mother's death.

My wife and I talked a lot. She listened to me. I had to come to terms with the fact that I either believed that this life wasn't the end of everything, or I didn't. My parents' deaths brought me face-to-face with this decision. I chose to believe in life after death, and that thought comforted me.

As sad as their deaths were, I knew that this wasn't the last time I would see my parents. On one hand, it was hard when Mom went; but on the other hand, it wasn't, because I had been through it before.

What made her passing difficult was that our little girl had just been born. I wanted Mom to have a long time with Angela, but that wasn't to be. Angela was only a few weeks old and had just smiled at Mom on the Friday before Mom died. I was grateful they had that much time together.

My mom's death wasn't so much my loss. It was the loss of the time our eldest daughter, Angela, had with her. Our second daughter, Lana, didn't even know her at all. My grief had shifted, and it was different. I was sad that they'd never know my mother. My grief had expanded from just me to my family.

Because Mom had been ill, her death wasn't like Dad's. It wasn't the crisis. It wasn't the shock. It felt too soon for her to go, but she had been through a lot of illnesses, so we weren't surprised.

With Mom, death came in a more traditional way. My wife and I dealt with it. We talked through our feelings. We were sad, but we pulled together. We made the funeral arrangements. We grieved at the services, and then we started healing. It was a more normal situation than with my dad.

The hard thing for me with my dad was that I didn't really have anyone to rely on or talk to at that time. I had some friends, but they were just guys. They didn't know. They hadn't been through anything like that and didn't know how to help. I didn't feel like I could talk to Mom. It was hard enough for her as it was. It was a very lonely time for me. When my mom passed, I had the support that I needed.

My brother, Jerry, was an alcoholic, a recluse, and a chain smoker. He lived alone in the old family home after Mom died. One night, he had too much to drink and fell asleep with a cigarette in his hand. He died in the house fire. He just never woke up.

Jerry's situation was different from the loss of either of my parents because I knew how hard life had been for him. He just struggled with life—period. Lana probably doesn't remember him very well, but Angela does. They had a relationship, and it was sad to have him gone. Again, my grief included not only me but also my family. I worried about how they were going to handle it more than anything.

But for Jerry, I knew that he would actually be happier now that he was not here anymore. I took comfort from that.

With Jerry's passing, neither my wife nor I can think about the specifics of it. Sometimes, you just have to push that out of your head. The state he was in and the situation the house was in—all burned.

Here is another difficult part of Jerry's death: We had a dear neighbor that lived just up the hill from the old family home. She was like a second mother to me while I was growing up. She saw the house burning and called the fire department. The police wouldn't let her call me, though.

It was a shock to have the police come to my door to tell me the news. (We lived several states away.) It would have been better for me to hear about it from my second mother than from the police. There was a grief counselor that came with the police officer. It was a kind thing to do. They wanted to make sure if I needed to talk there was someone there. I thanked them, but I wanted to talk to our neighbor.

Right after the police left our house, I called our neighbor, and she told me everything. She was the one I wanted to talk to—to be sad with.

Of all of the losses in our family, Dad's death was the most difficult to deal with. The other deaths were not easy, but less difficult because I had my wife and others to talk to for support.

So much has happened in my life since Dad died that I don't even think about it as often. With Mom, I think about her more. They say that time heals, and it really does.

Time doesn't ever take it away entirely, but you cope better. I find other things to focus on. I look for other things to be happy about and to be excited about, so that makes the difference.

I spent six months with a therapist who helped me put my life in perspective. I love to write so I have used my experiences in my stories. Now I have a better view of life and death, and it has taught me just how important my relationships are. I don't think I appreciated them before like I do now.

I have good memories about both my parents. We tell the girls about them. We keep their memories alive. Now we reminisce, and it's positive.

I think about the different ways each one in my family died. With my dad, it's like I just haven't seen him for a while. It's not like he's gone.

It was not the same with Mom, because we did see her in the casket. I was thinking about this a while ago and trying to decide which one is better. I'm not sure either is better.

With a closed casket, someone could say they didn't get to say goodbye and there was unfinished business. On the other hand, with the open casket, someone could say, "I wish I hadn't seen her this way." So really, I don't know if here is a right way or a wrong way to do it. Your grief is going to be there either way.

There were gifts through each of the tragedies. I just had to learn to recognize them:

- My pastor helped me.
- I was able to support my mother.
- My faith in God has deepened.
- I know there is life after this one.
- My mother had a chance to know our eldest daughter.
- My wife is my best friend.
- I want my children to know my family—even just through my memories.
- I have a strong family connection.
- The police were kind and helpful.
- My second mother was there for me.
- I can find the good in my life, no matter what happens.
- I am stronger because of what I've gone through.

CHAPTER 28

Finding a Therapist

Our tears are precious, necessary, and part of
what make us such endearing creatures.
—David Richo, *The Five Things We Cannot Change*

We have outlined a lot of self-healing techniques that will bring peace to your life, but you may want the support of a therapist during this difficult time of your life. Counselors have been trained to help you gain the coping skills you need to improve your life.

However, some people are not interested in therapy. There are many ways to heal, as outlined in the preceding pages. There is no right or wrong in the curative process. Find the way that works best for you and follow you heart in this most personal journey.

In this chapter, though, I want to share a few stories of clients who benefitted from therapy.

Heather came to counseling because she was depressed. Her self-esteem was low, and she had nothing good to say about herself. We worked through her childhood trauma, and she learned some positive-thinking techniques during our counseling sessions. I saw her twenty years later at a convention. She told me our work together had changed her life. She was very grateful.

I saw Tess, a young girl I worked with about ten years ago at the time of this writing, at a women's conference. Amy's stepdad was a voyeur, peeping at her through her bedroom window as she dressed and undressed. Amy worked through her issues, and we talked about healthy relationships. Amy's mom divorced the stepdad when he wasn't willing to address his addiction or be responsible for his problems. Amy has since finished her schooling, married, and has several children herself. She said how grateful she was for the things she learned in therapy.

A middle-aged man, Loran, had been molested as a young boy by a teen in his family. Loran struggled with same-sex attraction. He married and had a family because it was the "right" thing to do. Now he wanted to overcome his urges and stay with his wife and children because he loved them. As we worked together, he could see the skewed sexualization that developed early in his life because of the abuse. During therapy, he allowed himself to rehearse his early trauma and rewrite some of his childhood behaviors. Because of the work he put in through therapy, he moved on to healthier thinking patterns. I met him several years later at a marketing meeting. He reported that his sexual attraction for his wife fulfilled them both.

A therapist can help you work through the aftermath of a traumatic experience. Therapists focus on allowing you to release the hurt you have experienced. With their training, they will help you reframe your negative thinking so you can focus on the positive about you.

The following are a few rebuttals people give for not going to therapy:

I don't need a therapist if I need to talk. My family and friends will listen to my problems.

If you have experienced a tragedy in your life, those around you probably feel some emotional pain right along with you.

Family and friends can be a great sounding board for your troubles, but they can also become over-involved in your situation, giving you advice rather than letting you solve your own problem.

On the other hand, a therapist will listen to your situation, help you see the patterns in your behavior, and aid you in brainstorming possible solutions so you can make your own decision. A therapist can help you look at your life with some objectivity that your loved ones don't have.

Therapy is for whiners and complainers.

Therapy is hard work. Therapists are trained to find the root of your hurt. They can give you an outside perspective, help you look for solutions, and show you a way to live a more peaceful life.

Therapy is for crazy people.

You don't have to be diagnosed with a mental illness to benefit from therapy. I had many clients who came to therapy because they were having relationship problems or felt a lack of self-esteem. Some came seeking answers for their job stress or needed help with wayward teens. When you have experienced a tragedy or trauma, therapy is a good way to sort out your feelings and find relief.

I'm depressed; I'll just ask my doctor to give me a pill so I'll feel better.

Medication can be very helpful for anxiety and depression, but pills can't help solve your problems or help you pick up the pieces after tragedy strikes.

The length of therapy will vary, according to the problems to be addressed and according to the wishes of the client. Insurance payments have a lot to do with the time a person is in therapy. Talk with your therapist and work out a program together that fits your needs.

Finding a good therapist may seem like an overwhelming, scary task. Here are some ideas to help you begin the process.

1. Check with your insurance provider. If you choose someone on the list, your insurance will help with the cost. It may not pay the entire amount, but it will help.
2. Your tragedy may be covered by state or government funding. If this is the case, find out the particulars and participate as you wish.
3. Check the licensure of the therapist to make sure they are credible.
   a. Psychiatrists are medical doctors that provide medications but don't do a lot of counseling.
   b. Psychologists hold a doctorate's degree in psychology and are trained in all aspects of human behavior, psychology, and testing.
   c. Licensed clinical social workers hold a master's degree and work with families, couples, and individuals.
   d. Licensed marriage and family therapists hold a master's degree and work with families, couples, and individuals.
   e. Licensed professional counselors hold a master's degree and work with all kinds of behavioral problems.

   f. Licensed addiction counselors hold a bachelor's degree and work with addicts.
4. Find someone in your area. Traveling long distances can become a hassle, especially if you are dealing with traumatic circumstances.
5. Call each therapist on your list and ask for a short, fifteen-minute consultation. I was always glad to talk with potential clients on the phone or meet with them in person so they could decide if I would be a good fit for them.
6. Word of mouth is also a good way to find a counselor you like. Your friends or other trauma survivors may be able to recommend someone who has helped them.
7. Find a therapist who understands your culture and your religious beliefs. That can be vitally important as you look for help in healing and making decisions for your future.
8. Go with your intuition. Choose the person that seems right for you.

Find someone who:
- Will listen.
- Is caring.
- Is understanding.
- Talks about your feelings.
- Is accepting.

  Here is a list of websites to help you locate psychologists and therapists in your area. I wish you the best in this process.
  http://www.goodtherapy.org/find-therapist.html
  https://therapists.psychologytoday.com
  http://treatment.adaa.org
  http://www.find-a-therapist.com
  http://locator.apa.org

Summary

Therapists can be of great help in your healing process. They have specific skills in listening, finding emotional patterns, and looking at life from an objective perspective. Therapists can help you find the best in yourself and look for the strengths you didn't know you had.

Go through the list of providers in your area that you have singled out from your insurance, friends and family, and government agencies. Call each and interview them. Then choose the person you feel will be the kindest and most caring to help you with your tragedy.

Commitment

- Decide if therapy is right for you.
- Create a list of therapists you will consider seeing.
- Interview each one.
- Choose the person you feel is right for you.

CHAPTER 29

Group Work

"What happens when people open their hearts?"...
"They get better."
—Haruki Murakami, *Norwegian Wood*

Support groups can be a great benefit to those who have suffered a tragedy or are grieving the loss of a loved one. They provide an opportunity for us to share with others who know the road we are on. We are able to look at our pain in small doses and process the things we talk about each week. We grow from our own and others' experiences.

After the death of a loved one, our lives are changed forever. We must redefine our relationships and adjust to our new place in the world. As we complete this task, we come to know and appreciate life as we never have before. Because of our pain, our wisdom and understanding is increased, and we can share with those who have also experienced this awareness.

The objectives of support groups are to provide community, comradery, and friendships with people who understand and are at different stages of the same healing process. They are to help you and are for you to help in your turn. Let's look at some of the positive reasons for joining a support group.

Grief Group Positives

- **Sense of belonging**. When we have gone through trauma or loss, our sadness causes us to feel depressed, and we tend to isolate ourselves. Belonging to a group will take away that loneliness and feeling of seclusion.
- **A place of hopefulness.** In the initial stages of grief, we have no idea what this path will be like and what to expect. We meet with others who are further along this road, and it's nice to have someone who understands us and knows what lies ahead.
- **A place to be heard.** To have others listen to us is a great gift. As we share our stories, those around us will hear our pain and sadness. Listening brings with it the gift of healing. As this happens, we begin to find meaning in life again.
- **A place of kindness.** When we share our experience of pain and suffering, it's good to be with a group who will treat us with kindness and be nonjudgmental. They may give counsel—hopefully in a helpful way. And they will encourage us to be caring toward ourselves. Many of us feel guilty at the death of a loved one, for varied reasons. Self-compassion can be a big step in the healing process.
- **A place of counsel.** The group involvement will be filled with information, ideas, and suggestions as to how to go on with life. It's comforting to meet with people who know the way out of overwhelming sadness. It can be a place to help us find joy in life again.
- **A community of sharing.** When we are able to tell our experiences and share our wisdom, others will gain from our knowledge. As we heal and new people come into the group, we can help them along the path. The service we give to others strengthens us. When we truly heal, our gratitude guides us to give to others. The group process permits time to heal. Everyone's timetable for healing is different. The group helps one realize it's okay to take time for grief—whatever time is needed.

- **A place to explore the gifts that come from the healing process.** We learn compassion for ourselves and others. We find internal wisdom we didn't know we had. We are refined and polished as stones in the river.

Research findings show that the most effective groups have a common identity and a shared sense of purpose, per the *International Journal of Group Psychotherapy* in 2009.

Grief Group Negatives

- **A group can be overwhelming.** When we are just beginning our grieving process, meeting with others who feel the same way can be overwhelming. We not only see our own problems, but everyone else's difficulties. It can seem like too much.
- **Too much negativity.** If people in the group are negative, we can feel discouraged. If you find a group like this, look for another place to heal where those present take a positive stance. Those who share should be encouraged to be positive.
- **Judgmental participants.** There may be judgmental people in the group, so it may feel unsafe to share. Look for another group if this is the case. Your healing process is important. Find a group that meets your needs.
- **Cultural differences.** In your time of grief, find for a group that understands your culture. You need someone who appreciates you, your background, and your belief system. It's important to feel safe and understood.

Other Thoughts

Groups can be run by licensed therapists. In situations like this, group therapy can be as healing as individual counseling. These organizations tend to be safe and have added insight because they are run by a professional.

Groups can be facilitated by a hospice organization. They usually have trained facilitators also—maybe not therapists, but most hospice workers have extensive experience with death and dying and supporting the grieving family. They will make sure the group is safe and stays on task.

Religious organizations may also have grief groups. This could be a situation you are interested in because the people will have the same beliefs you do. Be sure to check out the group before you commit.

You want to feel secure and have the best healing situation possible.

Following is a short list of websites that will aid your healing process. Check out the resources in your community and find a grief group if you are interested.

Following is a website that has more than a hundred resources for grief groups and grief counseling.

https://www.mastersincounseling.org/loss-grief-bereavement.html

These are a few of the national websites listed on the Masters in Counseling site. Find a resource that will meet your needs.

Open to Hope: http://www.opentohope.com

The Sweeney Alliance: https://sweeneyalliance.org

National Alliance for Grieving Children: https://childrengrieve.org

Scholastic children's grief resources: http://www.scholastic.com/childrenandgrief

Tragedy Assistance Program for Survivors: http://www.taps.org

Suicide Grief: http://www.allianceofhope.org/alliance-of-hope-for-suic/support-groups.html

The National Child Traumatic Stress Network: https://www.nctsn.org

The National Center for Victims of Crime: http://www.victimsofcrime.org

Summary

Grief group work can be a tool for healing after trauma or the death of a loved one. It can be a place of belonging, a place to be heard, a place for counsel, a place of kindness, and a place to share wisdom and gifts that come from painful experiences.

Be cautious as you look for a group. Find one that is positive and will meet your needs. Above all, make sure it's a safe place for you to do your healing work.

Check your local resources and the national organizations listed on the internet and explore the options near you.

Commitment

- Check out local resources for grief groups
- Ask to attend a group just to check it out.
- Visit several groups before you make your choice.
- Attend the group that will best suit your needs.

CHAPTER 30

Gratitude

Piglet noticed that even though he had a Very Small Heart, it could hold a rather large amount of Gratitude.
—A. A. Milne, *Winnie-the-Pooh*

Gratitude has been an important part of my healing process. It's my go-to treatment plan whenever I am down. It brings me out of my negative thinking faster than anything else. Whenever I'm depressed, I begin repeating several gratitude mantras to pull myself out of my black hole. It gets my mind going in a positive direction.

At times, my negativity comes from anxiety and worry, and the mantras give me the peace I'm seeking. My mind listens to the grateful ideas I put in it and calms down. Another blessing associated with gratitude mantras is that it takes me to a place of humility where my mind becomes open to new ideas.

Robert Emmons and Michael McCullough, in the *Journal of Personality and Social Psychology*, studied counting blessings versus counting burdens and found those who focused on daily blessings were more optimistic, vigorous, pleasant, and better able to handle life's troubles.

Their sleep improved, and they were sick less often. They were more charitable and made greater progress toward their goals.

I used gratitude mantras extensively in my therapy practice. As with other healing methods we've explored, I let my clients write their own mantras. When I asked them what they wanted to write they usually responded with, "I don't know."

In that case, I waited them out. After thinking for a few minutes, they came up with one mantra, and then more and more.

Begin Your Daily Journal with a Thankful Statement

Psalm 116:12 reads, "What shall I render unto the Lord for all his benefits toward me?" (KJV)

This scripture is recorded at the beginning of my journal. I read it when I begin to write each entry. It sets my mind in an attitude of gratitude as I contemplate all that God has given me: the beauties of this earth, my warm place to live, my mind and body that aren't perfect but work well, the technology of the day, and especially the family I have been given.

I seem to be able to journal more clearly if I begin with a gratitude statement. It helps me focus when my mind is scattered, going off in many directions at once.

I always like to note the daily gifts I receive from working through my problems. If I do this, it keeps me from complaining and whining in my journal. It's also a good habit to get into, because when times get tough and tragedy happens, I'm already in the mode of finding the good during bad times.

What are your gifts?

Mine include these:

- Compassion
- Insight
- Empathy
- Understanding

Gratitude Journal

I had several clients that kept a specific gratitude journal apart from their daily writing. It was helpful for me to do the same while I was working through the anger at my father's death. I didn't continue keeping a separate gratitude journal after I finished therapy, but some people do. I include my gratitude in my daily journal.

Many of my clients found that their gratitude journal softened their approach to life. One severe abuse survivor let go of her hard shell of anger as she wrote about her gratitude. A little boy with low self-esteem recorded the things he was thankful for; it focused his thinking to look for the good in his life, and he began to feel better about himself.

Try it either way. See what is best for you.

Middle-of-the-Night Gratitude Mantras

Sometimes I wake in the night, not from bad dreams but just from worry. This happens when I am grieving, but also at other times. Anxiety can needle me awake for hours. The best way for me to go back to sleep is to repeat several mantras over and over.

"Darkness cannot drive out darkness: only light can do that."
　—Martin Luther King, Jr., *A Testament of Hope*

"Our life is frittered away by detail. . . . Simplify, simplify."
　—Henry David Thoreau, *Walden and Other Writings*

"I am thankful to be me.
Let go and let God."
　—Author Unknown

"Trust in the Lord with all thine heart; and lean not unto thine own understanding. In all thy ways acknowledge him, and he shall direct thy paths."
　—Proverbs 3:5–6 (KJV)

Gratitude Visualizations

Every morning when I meditate, I like to do a couple of gratitude visualizations. I always use things that I think will cross my path that day.

I love my roses. During the summer and fall, I wonder at the beauty of a rose—the colors, the delicate petals, the smell, the vibrancy of its life. No one can replicate their beauty.

We have a pear tree in the backyard. I pick and dry the pears to have for snacks and put in granola for winter. Then I can enjoy them all year long. I can see the beautiful yellow color of the ripe fruit, the soft white flesh, the dripping sugary juice, the way it melts on my tongue, and the smell as slices dry in my fruit drier on the back porch.

When the wind blows, the pines in our backyard whisper in the breeze. Pines smell deliciously like a forest. They are my giant protectors. I have watched them grow from small seedlings to large guardians of the backyard. If they can grow so straight and tall from small seedlings, then I know I can grow straight and tall as well.

Make up your own visualizations from things in your surroundings. We do have a beautiful world. If you need more inspiration or direction, look back through the chapters on visualization in part 2.

Gratitude Thoughts

In your busy day, take time for thankfulness—even for the person that irritates you at work. He keeps you humble. He's your reality check that you're not perfect—yet!

Today, I am grateful for my children. Each of them in their own way has taught me so many things. They have grown up with talents that are more developed than mine. They have taught me about hard work, patience, kindness, loving no matter what, and the joy of companionship. They have matured me, mellowed me, and made me the person I am today.

After a tragedy, we come to appreciate life more than we did before. We learn that life is fragile, and we are grateful for our lives and our friends and family. Read Marissa's story, "The Working World, 9/11 Survivor" at the beginning of part 1. After she survived the 9/11 attack, she felt more gratitude. She said *Thank you* more. She apologized more. She said *I love you* more. Gratitude became a greater part of her life after her tragedy.

Gratitude Lists

When I worked in therapy with children, I always asked them to tell me something good about themselves. In the beginning, most of them had a very hard time with that task. When they became better at it, I asked them to go a step further and find something about themselves they were grateful for.

It's a good exercise for us also. Which of your characteristics are you grateful for? Every night before you go to bed, think of three things about yourself that you are grateful for.

We might also include our physical bodies as well. I have a friend whose son was injured in a roadside bomb and lost his arm. Right now, I'm feeling grateful for my arms.

Gratitude is the heart's memory.
—Proverb

Gratitude is a sign of noble souls.
—Aesop

Summary

Keep gratitude at the forefront of your life. Those who include gratitude in their lives are healthier, sleep better, and have less illness than those who don't.

There are many ways to infuse your life with gratitude: meditation, journaling, mantras, and thankfulness lists. Choose what works for you and create your own program.

Commitment

- Include gratitude in your meditation time.
- Write a daily gratitude statement in your journal.
- Keep a separate gratitude journal if you wish.
- Find three good things about yourself that you are grateful for daily.

CHAPTER 31

Self-Compassion

*God, grant me the serenity to accept the things
    I cannot change,
Courage to change the things I can,
And wisdom to know the difference.*
                                    —Reinhold Niebuhr,
                        The National Council of Churches

After a tragic experience, we go back over the situation in our minds to think of what we could have done to avoid the trauma altogether, how we could have acted differently to save our loved one, what we could have done to stop the perpetrator, or whatever we could have done to keep the situation from happening.

We can't change the past. It would be wonderful if we could swoop in and save the day, but unfortunately, only Superman and Spider-Man are able to do that.

We must accept our humanness, including our shortcomings and foibles. We can't be all things to all people; it just isn't possible.

In the beginning of my marriage, I bent over backward to please my husband. I tried to make everything perfect for him and our three little girls. Because of my childhood feelings of abandonment, I took care of everyone but myself.

My girls saw this situation and each reacted in her own way. One grew up to be a caregiver. She does everything for others and takes care of herself last, patterning after my early behavior. Another daughter became overly assertive, wanting everything to go her way. The third daughter chose a partner who did not stay faithful to the marriage, playing out my issue of early childhood abandonment.

I feel sad about my behaviors in the early part of our marriage. I wish I could make things a little different for my girls, but that time is past. I have felt guilty for years over this situation and beat myself up over it, but the only thing that accomplishes is putting me into a state of depression.

How could I begin to let go of the past—find the courage to change the things I could and accept the things I couldn't? How could I learn to be kind to myself over this issue?

Self-compassion, according to Kristin Neff in her book *Self-Compassion*, includes practicing self-kindness, recognizing that we are all human and make mistakes, and becoming mindful of our place in life.

Here are some ways we can increase our self-compassion:

- **Notice:** I can notice the critical self-talk always in the back of my head. The feelings of inadequacy pile up with this kind of self-talk. For me, statements like, "You've ruined your children" only make things worse.

- **Soften the self-talk:** I can soften that negativity by looking for the good in my girls. They are wonderful people—all professional in their own right. They are good mothers and know what they stand for. I can say to myself, "Your children have a lot of goodness. They may have a few idiosyncrasies, but they are contributing members of society."

- **Hug:** I can give myself a hug. I can literally put my arms around myself in a physical embrace, caress my arms in a loving way, or use my creative visualization to mentor myself.

- **Creative Visualization:** Use your creative visualization (outlined in chapters 7, 8, and 9). Design a healing place and use your wise mentor as a guide or find a guardian-angel mother. Talk with your mentor about the negative voices inside your head. Listen to his or her advice as to how to soothe and heal them. Ask your mentor about caring for yourself and what that means in behavioral terms.

For me, it meant rehearsing all the positives in our children. My father (my wise mentor) reminded me about things I didn't see in my kids. My mentor and I worked together to bring me to a guilt-free place. (Well, most of the time.)

- **Accept our humanness:** We are all part of the human experience. Every one of us is imperfect, and we all make mistakes. We live in a competitive society where everyone tries to be the best—above average. We all know that's impossible. Everyone can't be above average. Can we stop comparing and judging ourselves? Let's look for the goodness that has come to us from our trials. Pray that everyone might come to accept their humanness and be kind to themselves. In doing this, we add light and love to the world. Even though others may not know we are praying for them, let's continue to do it.

- **Mindfulness:** We explored mindfulness in chapter 6. Use your mindfulness to experience each moment of critical self-talk. Sit with the critical statement and feelings. Be aware of the negativity it generates. You know you are not perfect, and it's okay. It's part of the human experience. Feel the sadness. Look at your self-talk and experience it, but know it isn't necessarily reality.

Add some loving-kindness to a meditation on self-compassion:
May I be peaceful.
May I be kind to myself.
May I be safe.

As you write the mantras for this meditation, add compassion for all the suffering in the world. Pray for everyone everywhere to find peace within themselves.

Kristin Neff has some wonderful guided mediations on self-compassion. Check out her website: http://self-compassion.org/category/exercises

- **Reframe:** Now reframe your emotions to see the good that surrounds your experience. Find the gifts that you take away from each of your trials. My girls became stronger because we have talked about my issues and where I was when they were little. I've apologized, and we've discussed better ways to build relationships. They can see the change in me, and they are developing in their own ways.

Adults often have an easier time than children recognizing where their self-compassion is lacking, because it is most often a cognitive process. For children, their processes are often intuitive, so they need support in learning to notice and reframe the self-talk. For example, when working with children who are facing the divorce of their parents, some of the negative messages are that their family is broken, that their parents didn't love them enough to stay together, or that they won't get their needs met.

When I work with a child in this circumstance, I let them express their fears and what they perceive as the new truths of their situation. Then, one by one, we work on positive reframes. These are some examples:

- "Now, I will have two families instead of one."
- "There will be twice as many people to love me."
- One little boy came up with the idea that he could get twice as many Christmas presents.

When these children can reframe the self-talk, their self-compassion is expanded and there is a big difference in their demeanor and how they can cope with potentially challenging circumstances.

Summary

Negative self-talk is ingrained in us from an early age. We are part of a competitive society that expects everyone to be above average. Be kind to yourself. Notice your critical thoughts. Soften them with positive statements. Have compassion for yourself. Use your creative visualization to get in touch with your wise mentor to access the light within you. Spend some mindful moments looking at your pain, your humanness, and your goodness. Reframe your trials by finding the gifts you have received from them.

Commitment

- Notice your negativity.
- Soften your self-talk.
- Hug yourself.
- Practice your creative visualization.
- Accept your humanness.
- Spend some mindful moments with peace each day.
- Write some kindness mantras.
- Find your gifts in life.

CHAPTER 32

Finding Peace amid Political Turmoil

Nonviolence does not mean nonaction. Nonviolence means we act with love and compassion. The moment we stop acting we undermine the principle of nonviolence.
—Thich Nhat Hahn, *Be Still and Know*

There has been war, lust for power, and political unrest throughout the ages of the world. One of the most infamous leaders was Genghis Khan, whose hardened, ruthless army swept through China and across Asia from the Mongolian steppe into Russia and Southeastern Europe, killing almost forty million people and leaving blood and carnage wherever it went.

Other names come to mind, such as Napoleon, who was responsible for approximately three and a half million dead. But that doesn't hold a candle to the World War II death toll, under the auspices of Hitler, which reached about sixty million.

We must ask ourselves what kind of beings we are to continue to perpetrate these atrocities on one another. It's one thing to list death tolls, which are just statistics and mean little to us. But when we think of fathers and mothers holding dead children in their arms and about to be slaughtered themselves, the picture becomes more personal and bleak. What kind of terror did these people feel as they faced death? What were their last moments like? What was their fear level? Their anxiety level? We can only imagine.

> I was a child, living in Holland at the time Hitler conquered my homeland. My parents were flooded with uncontrolled anxiety and feelings of helplessness. They worried about the future for me, their child, in the presence of such an enemy.
> —Ada Warner

Humans are survivors by nature. We all go through tough times. And when we do, there is an innate fight inside us to rise above our circumstances. Ada's parents and their children escaped to the United States from Holland and found a quality of life for their family.

> Everything can be taken from a man but one thing: the last of the human freedoms—to choose one's attitude in any given set of circumstances, to choose one's own way.
> —Viktor Frankl, *Man's Search for Meaning*

Viktor Frankl, a noted Austrian psychiatrist and Holocaust survivor, came out of his experience in Hitler's death camps to pose the theory that the only way man can survive the most despicable circumstances is to contemplate love. As Frankl trudged along a rocky, muddy road, being pressed and goaded by the rifle butts of his Nazi captors, he held an image of his beloved wife always in his mind. Keeping his love for his wife foremost in his awareness during these dark times gave meaning to his existence. In the death camps, he survived typhoid fever, the deaths of his wife, his mother, and his brother by searching for meaning in his life.

> Let us pick up our books and our pens.
> They are our most powerful weapons.
> —Malala Yousafzai

In 2009, Malala Yousafzai, a preteen Pakistani girl, gained notoriety when she wrote a blog for the BBC, outlining the existence of a child under the rule of the Taliban. She received further attention when her life became the subject of a *New York Times* documentary. As she climbed aboard a Pakistani school bus in 2012, she was shot in the face by a gunman. The incident sparked an international outpouring of support for her. After her recovery, she continued to fight tirelessly for the education of girls and youth and for women's rights. She has received worldwide acclaim, including many awards. In 2014, she was the co-recipient of a Nobel Peace Prize for her support of children's rights and the education of youth.

Terrorist groups are active not only in Pakistan but also in Syria, North Korea, Sudan, Libya, Iran, Iraq, and Cuba. Where will they strike next? One only has to read the newspaper each day to identify a new crisis somewhere in the world. We only need mention cities like London, Orlando, Berlin, New York, and Paris to pull up horrific memories of terror.

Even though these types of incidents may not affect us personally, we still experience the impact of them. How many of us felt afraid after the 9/11 attacks? Remember the sleep study done at Tufts University after that assault discussed in chapter 13? None of the people in that experiment had friends or family personally involved in 9/11, but following that tragedy, they experienced a significant increase in nightmares.

So it is with us. We are each affected by catastrophic events happening in the world today. We feel anxious and unsafe.

It's important for us to practice the techniques outlined in this book so that we can find peace in our lives even though we live in a troubled world. These include creative visualizations to a safe place, counseling with a wise mentor, practicing mindfulness and gratitude, and many more techniques. As we use the skills set forth in each chapter, we will improve our quality of life and find peace and joy in our personal world.

Many people in the United States are suffering because of current issues in our country. We have many unresolved problems. Struggles over political issues will probably always exist. How do we put the happenings of today into perspective? How will we choose to live our lives amid these issues?

What can we do to find peace in a troubled world? Let's remember Viktor Frankl's idea of keeping love at the forefront of our lives and looking for meaning in all that we do.

What is our role in making the world a better place? Just like Malala Yousafzai, we can stand up for change. Look for a way to add light and love to the world to make it a better place for all of us.

How do we do that? Let's go back to the quote by Thich Nhat Hahn, which opened this chapter. Nonviolence means action. We want change in a peaceful way. What kind of actions can we take that will improve the current situation?

- Serve in the community.
- Donate to charities that help the disadvantaged.
- Listen to minorities, and champion their cause.
- Join special-interest groups you believe in.
- Write letters to the editor of your local newspaper.
- Write letters to your elected officials. Tell them how you feel.
- Participate in your local caucus meetings.
- Participate in your state caucus meetings.
- Campaign for political candidates who support issues you believe in.
- Run for political office.

One child, one teacher, one book and
one pen can change the world.

—Malala Yousafzai

What do you tell your children after they have experienced tragedy? There are no cut-and-dried answers to this question. A lot depends on the nature of the child, their relationship to the tragedy, and several other factors. But there are some basic principles and steps that can help you teach your child the same skills you are practicing.

> It is impossible to escape the impression that people commonly use false standards of measurement—that they seek power, success and wealth for themselves and admire them in others, and that they underestimate what is of true value in life.
> —Sigmund Freud,
> *Civilization and Its Discontents*

> When the power of love overcomes the love of power, the world will know peace.
> —Jimi Hendrix

Maybe your child has questions about an earthquake halfway around the world that they've seen on television. Or they could have gone through the terror of a hurricane or tornado themselves. The difference in distance will cause children to have very different ideas.

The most important things for a parent to remember are these:

- Ask questions. Find out where the child is coming from.
- Listen to their fears and concerns. Don't give some big explanation about something they don't even care about.
- Address these feelings. Let the child talk through them.
- Provide some ideas for them to release these feelings:
  - Talking.
  - Journaling.
  - Art work in any form they choose.
  - Large-muscle activity like punching a pillow or playing soccer.
  - Encouraging them to choose activities that will be helpful.
- Reframe the tragedy so your child doesn't stay stuck in negative feelings. Help them create their own or start with some like these ideas:

- Look for the good all around. (Then show examples of how others help in the aftermath.)
- Light is always stronger than dark.
- Love is always greater than hate.
- We gain strength from our troubles.

We can never obtain peace in the world
if we neglect the inner world and don't
make peace with ourselves. World peace
must develop out of inner peace.

—Dalai Lama

When we address problems within our reach, we will gain strength to work through issues that seem beyond our grasp. Becoming proactive can help all of us face the immobilizing fears that are often present after tragedy.

Summary

Lust for power and control has led to war since the world began. Terrorism is still part of our world today. But there is an innate ability inside all of us to rise above our troubles. Viktor Frankl espoused that love will pull us through even the most difficult situations. Malala Yousafzai stood up for what she believed.

Look for ways you can make a difference in the world. Take action to give service in your community by letting your voice be heard.

Commitment
- Keep love at the forefront of your life.
- Search for meaning in all you do.
- Let your voice be heard.
- Add light to the world as you see fit.

The next chapter will outline some things we all can do to find inner peace in our lives.

CHAPTER 33

A Quick Pickup

"You have peace," the old woman said, *"when you make it with yourself."*

—Mitch Albom,
The Five People You Meet in Heaven

All of us have down days at times. These might be triggered by an external trauma, a curt remark by a family member, or maybe they just seem to happen for no reason at all. On these days, we need to have a routine that will help us pull ourselves out of the funk we are in so we can go about our day.

Here are several techniques that will help. Some of them we have talked about in other sections of the book, but all of them are good for fostering a peaceful, positive attitude.

Smile

Research has shown that smiling can change the chemistry in your brain just like an antidepressant. It's an instant antidote to despair. Scientific evidence also shows that others will perceive you as being more attractive, intelligent, and assertive. Smiling is an all-around positive to include in your life.

If you have a hard time remembering to smile, hold a pencil between your teeth. This action forces your smile muscles to operate and will give your brain a positive boost. Then, someone asks you why you have a pencil between your teeth, and voilà! You can explain the smiling concept to them, and you've just added positive energy to the world by giving your secret away to someone else.

So smile. It's the best antidepressant around.

Breathing

We talked about breathing in chapter 6 and in case studies from several other chapters.

Deep breathing can reduce your anxiety and stress. When I am aware of my breathing, it takes my mind off whatever I'm worrying about at the moment. It clears my head and flushes the anxiety from my body.

Slow and steady breathing can change your heart rate. Your heart will pump slightly faster as you breathe in, and it will slow down a little when you exhale. This type of breathing can lower your heart rate altogether.

Breathe in slowly to the count of four, then release your breath to the count of eight. Be aware of your breath, the magic of breathing, and feel gratitude for its life-giving properties.

Practice Mindfulness

In the space of one very deep, slow breath, you can apply five techniques to help you reduce your stress. You already know about smiling and deep breathing.

For me, the relaxation comes when I smile and breathe. Just put your attention on your body as a whole and let it relax as you breathe out. As you do that, focus attention on your body or something in the immediate environment.

As you notice your body and your surroundings, your attention is diverted from your worrying or anxious thinking.

Your mind may want to continue its worrying, but choose to keep your attention on your immediate experience. Then continue this diversion by choosing to focus on something constructive and positive.

Internalizing the Good

We all notice the good around us. A dog leaping for a Frisbee in the park. A mother hugging her child. A sailboat whooshing across the water. A beautiful field of daffodils.

Take a little time with each positive image you come upon. Spend ten or twelve seconds with a mindful moment. Enjoy it. Soak it in. Each of these upbeat pauses can pull us from the negative into a positive state.

Make it a habit to dwell on the good, as suggested by Rick Hanson in *Hardwiring Happiness*. As he notes in his book, this old folk wisdom has been scientifically researched and MRI scans show this practice can change the structure of our brains.

Mantras

We discussed mantras in chapter 24. Remember, they are repeated phrases or messages of truth. These can be your own personal mantras or wise words from authors you admire.

I find it useful to create my own mantra or use one I already like that will counteract whatever my negative thoughts are saying. Just take a deep breath and come up with a few words that can be said or thought in the space of the next breath. Say the words mindfully over and over. It's soothing to repeat the message.

- God, help me find peace.
- May my heart be filled with loving-kindness (forgiveness, compassion).

Contemplative Prayer

Begin with your deep breathing to settle your mind. Let your thoughts come and go, but watch for meaningful words that float in and out of your mind in your spiritual quest. When you find words that resonate with you, repeat them silently and mindfully. Be aware of the feeling tone they generate. You can also use visuals. Here are some possible words: *peace, kindness, love, caring, God, kinship, warmth, joy, wisdom, courage*, and *strength*.

Following is a loving-kindness meditation prayer:

1. Begin with yourself. ("May I be happy. May I find peace.")
2. Be thankful for someone who has been kind to you. ("May you be happy.")
3. Show gratitude for a person you feel neutral about.

4. Give thanks for someone you dislike.

5. Bless the world. ("May everyone throughout the world find peace.")

May we all find peace and spiritual energy in this time of trouble. May we use our energy, intelligence, and talents to see clearly and invigorate our values. May we find deeper meaning and purpose in our lives. Amen.

Candy Gunther Brown, PhD, outlines sources for further study in *Psychology Today*: https://www.psychologytoday.com/blog/testing-prayer/201411/mindfulness.

Even though the chapter has been outlined as a short-term solution to anxiety and depression, this material is for long-term use. It's a daily tune-up that will keep us at our best, whether we are in the midst of tragedy or not.

Summary

Whether you are looking for a quick fix for a down day or you need a long-term program to feel positive, the following steps are an excellent start to each day: Smile to bring up your mood. Deep-breathing exercises can reduce anxiety and clear your mind. Notice your positive surroundings and take a mindful moment to experience the joy associated with them. Mantras and prayer can bring peace to your soul and lead you out of yourself to focus on the good in the world around you.

Commitment

Make the following a part of your daily routine:

- Smile.
- Breathe.
- Smile, breathe, relax, notice, choose.
- Internalize the good.
- Create mantras.
- Practice contemplative prayer.

CHAPTER 34

My Spirituality

The greatest disease in the West today is not TB or leprosy; it is being unwanted, unloved, and uncared for. . . . It is not only a poverty of loneliness but also of spirituality. There's a hunger for love, as there is a hunger for God.
—Mother Teresa, *Mother Teresa: A Simple Path*

Spirituality can be seen as a connection with ourselves, others, the life around us, and God. As we seek to define and build these relationships, we find purpose in life. My spirituality may be different from yours, but I share a few examples of how spiritual connection has affected me, my clients, and the authors mentioned in this chapter to offer a perspective and a pattern that can be adapted to fit all faiths.

A relationship with God, or a higher power, has been part of civilizations since the world began. Do we look to our higher power to rescue us from our problems? Or do we allow our trials is to bring us closer to God?

Some of the stories in this book have shown the resilience people can choose after tragedy by coming closer to God because of their misfortunes. In the face of trials, what will your choice be? Will you choose faith, hope, and a connection with your spirituality? Connect with your higher power so you hear His desires for you. Let this be part of your inner wisdom.

Carl Jung, an early psychologist, believed that spirituality is becoming our very best self—our connection with ourselves. He called this path of polishing and refining individuation and looked on it as the heart of all religions. He defined it as a voyage to meet our divine center.

After the death of a loved one, our relationship with them changes. We go through a redefining of ourselves and our connection to the person who has passed on. As I mentioned earlier in the book, I cared for my grandmother in our home until her death. After she passed away, I felt like I had lost a child—my baby was gone. (Near the end of her life, I bathed, diapered, dressed, and fed her.)

I had to readjust myself to my loss. After her death, my memories and experiences with her were not gone. They remain part of my life. Even though she passed away quite a few years ago, there are still times when she is in my thoughts and my creative visualizations. She is part of my spirituality—my connection to this life and the life to come.

Immediately after the death of a loved one, we may feel as if we've fallen into a dark hole that we cannot climb out of. Our spiritual beliefs can be the lifeline that pulls us from our abyss. It is possible for a connection with the divine to lift us from the darkness of our grief. Because of my trust in an afterlife, I know I will see my grandmother again. I look forward to that day.

Notice that in our spirituality and our relationships with God, friends, and family, the connection is the significant principle that aids us in our grieving process.

Service is also part of my spirituality. I strengthen my love for my higher power and others as I give of my time to make the world a better place. Jeremy (see "Two Daughters, The Same Brain Tumors" at the beginning of part 2) was angry after the death of his two girls, but he continued to give service to his church, even in the face of his resentment and grief. As he served, his anger dissipated and he found peace.

Life after the trauma can become a time of rediscovery of our life in relationship to God, those around us, and the world in general. As we turn to God for comfort, we might need to address the following questions:

- Who am I?
- Where did I come from?
- Is there life after death?
- Where will I go after this life?
- Is life eternal?

Theron came face-to-face with these questions after his father committed suicide.

Spirituality, or even religion, will never be able to give us back the association with our loved one as it previously was. Nor will they take away the trauma in our lives. There is never a shortcut through the grief process. However, there can be comfort. We must ask ourselves: What gifts can we gain from our trials? Can we help someone else who has suffered the same as we have?

> Nothing that you have not given
> away will ever be really yours.
> —C. S. Lewis, *Mere Christianity*

As we look at the refining process that comes from tragedy, I think C. S. Lewis gave us a metaphor that we all can identify with:

> Imagine yourself as a living house. God comes in to rebuild that house. At first, perhaps, you can understand what He is doing. He is getting the drains right and stopping the leaks in the roof and so on; you knew that those jobs needed doing and so you are not surprised. But presently He starts knocking the house about in a way that hurts abominably and does not seem to make any sense. What on earth is He up to? The explanation is that He is building quite a different house from the one you thought of—throwing out a new wing here, putting on an extra floor there, running up towers, making courtyards. You thought you were being made into a decent little cottage: but He is building a palace. He intends to come and live in it Himself. —C. S. Lewis, *Mere Christianity*

While not the most comfortable process, having trust in your spirituality, no matter how it looks, provides context and perspective to your journey. Trust your path in life.

> Knowing others is intelligence;
> knowing yourself is true wisdom.
> Mastering others is strength;
> mastering yourself is true power.
> —Lao Tzu, *Tao Te Ching*

Summary

Commit to improving your relationship with yourself, your family and friends, and your higher power. Look for spiritual connections in your life. Foster your own inner wisdom and growth. Discover your purpose and meaning in life. After a loss, use your spirituality as a lifeline to pull you across the abyss of grief.

Find the gifts that result from your trauma. Be grateful for all you have and share that gratitude with others. Find something loving to do for others every day.

The goodness and loving generosities of the world are all around you. Connect with them so that they can fortify you in times of trauma and tragedy. May the bounties of the earth be yours as you seek to find your peace. Give service. Share with others and you will be filled with abundance.

Commitment

- Include spirituality in your life.
- Let your spirituality pull you out of your grief.
- Discover your purpose in life.
- Practice doing things that bring meaning to your existence.
- Seek answers to questions about your existence.
- Show appreciation for those around you.
- Be mindful of every precious moment you live.
- Love others without expecting anything in return.

Conclusion

Writing this book has been a pleasure. It has been therapeutic for me to revisit the tragedies in my own life and the impact they've had on my life and that of my family. Someone once asked me if I had finished grieving for my father. I don't know what it means to be finished with the grief process. Does it mean I don't feel sad and miss him at times? I do miss him. We still spend time together. I continue to discuss things with him in my creative visualizations. Does it mean I don't carry the deep ache in my heart that used to be there? That has gone. I am not burdened by the pain anymore. I have mourned my loss.

Now I enjoy all the goodness that my father and I had together. I've made it part of my present life. Many gifts have blessed my existence from his death. I am a more thoughtful person, a wiser individual, and an empathetic being because I suffered this loss.

My best wishes go with each of you as you grieve your tragedy, sort through your pain, and release it. My hope for you is that you will find the goodness and blessings that have come into your life from misfortune.

May life give you an abundance of peace and love. May you find rich blessings in your pursuits of life. May your higher power go with you in all you do.

Bibliography

Chapter 2: Symptoms and Feelings We Experience When Tragedy Strikes

American Psychiatric Association. *Diagnostic and Statistical Manual of Mental Disorders*. 5th ed. Washington, DC: American Psychiatric Publishing, 2013.

Pennebaker, J. W. "Writing About Emotional Experiences as a Therapeutic Process." *Psychological Science* 8, no. 3 (May 1997): 162–66. 10.1111/j.1467-9280.1997.tb00403.x.

Chapter 3: Healing Is a Process

Kübler-Ross, Elisabeth, and David Kessler. *On Grief and Grieving: Finding the Meaning of Grief Through the Five Stages of Loss*. New York: Scribner, 2007.

Chapter 4: Tragedy and the Brain

Bremner, J. D. "Traumatic Stress: Effects on the Brain." *Dialogues in Clinical Neuroscience* 8, no. 4 (December 2006): 445–61.

Bremner, J. D., B. Elzinga, C. Schmahl, and E. Vermetten. "Structural and Functional Plasticity of the Human Brain in Posttraumatic Stress Disorder." *Progress in Brain Research* 167 (2008): 171–86. 10.1016/S0079-6123(07)67012-5.

Matta, Christy. *The Stress Response*. Oakland: New Harbinger, 2012.

Mayo Clinic. "Enhance Healing Through Guided Imagery." *ScienceDaily*. January 7, 2008. <www.sciencedaily.com/releases/2008/01/080104123246.htm>.

Rosenthal, Michele. *Heal Your PTSD: Dynamic Strategies That Work*. San Francisco: Conari, 2015.

Chapter 5: Tragedy and the Body

Vaccaro, Gaetano, and Joni Lavick. "Trauma: Frozen Moments, Frozen Lives." *The Body*. Summer 2008. http://www.thebody.com/content/art48754.html#immediate.

Chapter 6: Listening to Yourself

Baginski, Caren. "3 Yoga Breathing Exercises for Anxiety." YouTube, January 18, 2015. Video, 7:24. https://www.youtube.com/watch?v=N9jmO6xwFfs.

Hoge, E. A., E. Bui, L. Marques, C. A. Metcalf, L. K. Morris, D. J. Robinaugh, J. J. Worthington, M. H. Pollack, and N. M. Simon. "Randomized Controlled Trial of Mindfulness Meditation for Generalized Anxiety Disorder: Effects on Anxiety and Stress Reactivity." *Journal of Clinical Psychiatry* 74, no. 8 (2013): 786–92. 10.4088/JCP.12m08083.

Harris, Russ. *ACT Made Simple*. New Harbinger Made Simple Series. Oakland: New Harbinger, 2009.

Harris, Russ. *The Happiness Trap*. Boston: Trumpeter Books, 2008.

Harris, Russ. "Mindfulness without Meditation." *Healthcare, Counselling and Psychotherapy Journal* 9, no. 4 (October 2009): 21–24. https://www.actmindfully.com.au/upimages/Mindfulness_without_meditation_--_Russ_Harris_--_HCPJ_Oct_09.pdf.

Hayes, Steven. "About ACT." *ACBS*. Accessed September, 23, 2016. https://contextualscience.org/about_act.

Hayes, Steven C., Kirk D. Strosahl, Kelly G. Wilson. *Acceptance and Commitment Therapy: The Process and Practice of Mindful Change*. 2nd ed. New York: Guilford, 2012.

Kand, Erick. "Anxiety and Stress Relief with Diaphragmatic Breathing." YouTube, February 2, 2016. Video, 19:51. https://www.youtube.com/watch?v=pKZCGVxman.

Livingstone, Meghan. "3 Deep Breathing Exercises to Reduce Stress and Anxiety." YouTube, April 29, 2016. Video, 7:59. https://www.youtube.com/watch?v=sJ04nsiz_M0.

Chapter 7: Healing the Whole Person

Schwartz, Jeffrey M., and Rebecca Gladding. *You Are Not Your Brain: The 4-Step Solution for Changing Bad Habits, Ending Unhealthy Thinking, and Taking Control of Your Life*. New York: Avery, 2012.

Siegel, Daniel J. *Mindsight: The New Science of Personal Transformation*. New York: Bantam Books, 2010.

Chapter 8: Creative Visualizations—An Internal Guide

"Enhance Healing through Guided Imagery." Science Daily. January 7, 2008. https://www.sciencedaily.com/releases/2008/01/080104123246.htm.

Monson, Christy. *Becoming Free: A Woman's Guide to Internal Strength*. Sanger, CA: Familius, 2013.

Chapter 10: Body Work and Trauma

van der Kolk, Bessel. *The Body Keeps the Score: Brain, Mind, and Body in the Healing of Trauma*. New York: Penguin Books, 2015.

Zschucke, Elisabeth, Katharina Guadlitz, and Andres Ströhle. "Exercise and Physical Activity in Mental Disorders: Clinical and Experimental Evidence." Supplement, *Journal of Preventive Medicine and Public Health* 46 (Supplement 1; January 2013): S12–S21. 10.3961/jpmph.2013.46.S.S12.

Chapter 12: Grief and Disconnected Feelings

Chapman, Benjamin P., Kevin Fiscella, Ichiro Kawachi, Paul Duberstein, and Peter Muennig. "Emotion Suppression and Mortality Risk Over a 12-Year Follow-Up." *Journal of Psychosomatic Research* 75, no. 4 (October 2013): 381–85. https://doi.org/10.1016/j.jpsychores.2013.07.014.

Chapter 13: Nightmares

American Psychiatric Association. *Diagnostic and Statistical Manual of Mental Disorders*. 5th ed. Washington, DC: American Psychiatric Publishing, 2013.

Harmon, Katherine. "The Changing Mental Health Aftermath of 9/11—Psychological 'First Aid' Gains Favor over Debriefings." *Scientific American*, September 10, 2011.

http://www.scientificamerican.com/article/the-changing-mental-health/.

Heffron, Thomas. "What We Can Learn from 9/11 about Dreams and Nightmares." *Sleep Education*. September, 11, 2013. http://www.sleepeducation.org/ news/2013/09/11/what-we-can-learn-from-9-11-about-dreams-and-nightmares.

Hartmann, Ernest, and Tyler Brezler. "A Systematic Change in Dreams after 9/11/01." *Sleep* 31, no. 2 (2008): 213–218. https://www.ncbi.nlm.nih.gov/pmc/articles/ PMC2225570/.

Chapter 15: Anger

"Anger: Grief's Irate Companion." Beliefnet. http://www.beliefnet.com/wellness/ health/health-support/grief-and-loss/2000/10/anger-griefs-irate-companion. aspx#algJHtY1lzj2wozf.99.

Fitzgerald, Helen. *The Mourning Handbook*. New York: Fireside, 1994.

Kübler-Ross, Elisabeth, and David Kessler. *On Grief and Grieving: Finding the Meaning of Grief Through the Five Stages of Loss*. New York: Scribner, 2007.

"5 Steps to Let Go of Anger for a Happier Life." *Tiny Buddha*. http://tinybuddha.com/ blog/5-steps-to-let-go-of-anger-for-a-happier-life/ (page discontinued).

Chapter 16: Forgiveness

Gandhi, Mahatma. *All Men Are Brothers: Autobiographical Reflections*. London: Continuum, 1980.

Hanson, Rick. *Hardwiring Happiness: The New Brain Science of Contentment, Calm, and Confidence*. New York: Harmony Books, 2013.

Harris, A. H. S., F. Luskin, S. B. Norman, S. Standard, J. Bruning, S. Evans, and C. E. Thoresen. "Effects of a Group Forgiveness Intervention on Forgiveness, Perceived Stress and Trait Anger." *Journal of Clinical Psychology* 62, no. 6 (June 2006): 715–33. https://doi.org/10.1002/jclp.20264.

Lawler, Kathleen A., Jarred W. Younger, Rachel L. Piferi, Rebecca L. Jobe, Kimberley A. Edmondson, and Warren H. Jones. "The Unique Effects of Forgiveness on Health: An Exploration of Pathways." *Journal of Behavioral Medicine* 28, no. 2 (April 2005): 157–67.

Swartz, Karen. "Forgiveness: Your Health Depends on It." *Johns Hopkins Medicine*. http://www.hopkinsmedicine.org/health/healthy_aging/healthy_connections/ forgiveness-your-health-depends-on-it.

Toussaint, Loren, Grant S. Shields, Gabriel Dorn, and George M. Slavich. "Effects of Lifetime Stress Exposure on Mental and Physical Health in Young Adulthood: How Stress Degrades and Forgiveness Protects Health." *Journal of Health Psychology* 21,no. 6 (June 2016): 1004–14. https://doi.org/10.1177/ 135910531454432.

Chapter 17: Letter to Your Loved One

Pennebaker, James. *Writing to Heal: A Guided Journal for Recovering from Trauma and Emotional Upheaval*. Oakland: New Harbinger Publications, 2004.

"Processing Grief Through Writing Letters." The Center for Growth. http://www. therapyinphiladelphia.com/tips/processing-grief-through-writing-letters.

Chapter 18: Grief and the Creative Arts

Carson, Shelley. *Your Creative Brain*. San Francisco: Jossey-Bass, 2010.

"The Evolving Emotions of Grief: An Art Journal Activity for Grievers." *What's*

Your Grief? Last modified April 12, 2017. http://www.whatsyourgrief.com/
grief-art-journal-activity-for-grievers/.
Neimeyer, R. A. "Reauthoring Life Narratives: Grief Therapy as Meaning
Reconstruction." *Israel Journal of Psychiatry and Related Sciences* 38, nos. 3–4
(2001): 171–83.
Pennebaker, J. (2000) "Telling Stories: The Health Benefits of Narrative." *Literature
and Medicine* 19, no. 1 (Spring 2000): 3–18. 10.1353/lm.2000.0011.
Devine, Megan. "Pain Is Not Redeemed by Art: Grief, Loss and Creative Practice."
Huffington Post. Updated May 16, 2014. http://www.huffingtonpost.com/megan-
devine/pain-is-not-redeemed-by-a_b_4976261.html.
Linnehan, Christine. "Beyond Words: A Creative Arts Approach to Counseling the
Bereaved." *ADEC Forum* 39, no. 4 (October 2013): 1, 4–6. http://www.krsf.com/
pdf/adec-forum-oct-13-the-art-of-condolence.pdf.
Schlitz, Marilyn. *Death Makes Life Possible.* Boulder, CO: Sounds True, 2015.

Chapter 19: Body Work and Grieving

Fehrs, Linda. "Muscle Memory, Trauma and Massage Therapy." Institute for
Integrative Healthcare. August 1, 2013. http://www.integrativehealthcare.org/mt/
archives/2013/08/muscle-memory-trauma-and-massage-therapy.html.
LeBlanc, N. J., L. D. Unger, and R. J. McNally. "Emotion and Physiological Reactivity
in Complicated Grief." *Journal of Affective Disorders* 94 (April 2016): 98–104.
10.1016/j.jad.2016.01.024.

Chapter 20: Mistaken Childhood Beliefs and the Grieving Process

Corey, Elisabeth. "Grieving My Lost Childhood." *Psych Central.* Accessed
November 28, 2017. http://psychcentral.com/blog/archives/2013/07/29/
grieving-my-lost-childhood/.
Williams, Monnica T. "Overcoming the Pain of Childhood Abuse and Neglect:
Finding Our Way through Upsetting Memories." *Psychology Today.* March 14,
2013. https://www.psychologytoday.com/blog/culturally-speaking/201303/
overcoming-the-pain-childhood-abuse-and-neglect.

Chapter 21: Biography

Feiler, Bruce. "The Stories That Bind Us." *New York Times.* March 15, 2013. http://
www.nytimes.com/2013/03/17/fashion/the-family-stories-that-bind-us-this-life.
html?_r=0.
Grinyer, Anne. "The Narrative Correspondence Method: What a Follow-Up Study
Can Tell Us about the Longer Term Effect on Participants in Emotionally
Demanding Research." *Qualitative Health Research.* 14, no. 10 (December 1,
2004): 1326–41. https://doi.org/10.1177/1049732304269674.
Grinyer, Anne. "Telling the Story of Illness and Death." *Auto/Biography* 14, no. 3
(September 2006): 206–222. 10.1191/0967550706ab041oa.
Neimeyer, Robert A., ed. *Techniques of Grief Therapy: Creative Practices for
Counseling the Bereaved.* New York: Routledge, 2012.
Norton, Michael I., and Francesca Gino. "Rituals Alleviate Grieving for Loved Ones,
Lovers, and Lotteries." *Journal of Experimental Psychology: General* 143, no. 1
(February 2014). Advance online publication, February 11, 2013. http://www.
people.hbs.edu/mnorton/norton%20gino.pdf. 10.1037/a0031772.

Chapter 22: A Memorial Tribute

Johnson, Judith. "Honoring the Memory of a Deceased Loved One." *Huffington Post*. Updated November 17, 2011. http://www.huffingtonpost.com/judith-johnson/ the-power-of-bearing-witn_1_b_736710.html.

Chapter 23: Positive Thinking

Frank, Anne. *Diary of a Young Girl*. Reissue ed. New York: Bantam Books, 1993.

Gino, Francesca, and Michael I. Norton. "Why Rituals Work." Scientific American. May 14, 2013. Accessed June 06, 2018. https://www.scientificamerican.com/ article/why-rituals-work/.

Hanson, Heidi. "Why It's Difficult to 'Think Positive!' When You Have PTSD." *The Art of Healing Trauma: Illustrated Trauma Healing Exercises, Stories and Research*. April 28, 2015. http://www.new-synapse.com/aps/wordpress/?p=956.

Hanson, Rick. *Hardwiring Happiness: The New Brain Science of Contentment, Calm, and Confidence*. New York: Harmony Books, 2013.

Platt, Melissa, and Jennifer Freyd. "Trauma and Negative Underlying Assumptions in Feelings of Shame: An Exploratory Study." *Psychological Trauma: Theory, Research, Practice, and Policy* 4, no. 4 (2012): 370–78. http://dx.doi.org/10.1037/a0024253.

Substance Abuse and Mental Health Services Administration. *Trauma-Informed Care in Behavioral Health Services*. Treatment Improvement Protocol Series 57. HHS Publication No. (SMA) 13-4801. Rockville, MD: Substance Abuse and Mental Health Services Administration, 2014.

Chapter 24: Personal Mantras

Herbert, Frank. *Dune*. Ace Special 25th Anniversary ed. New York: Ace, 1990.

"How to Create Your Own Personal Mantra." *Oprah.com*. June 23, 2016. http://www. oprah.com/inspiration/How-to-Create-Your-Own-Personal-Mantra.

Joyce, James, quoted in Jacky Sachs, comp., *The Book of Blessings*.Kennebunkport, ME: Cider Mill Press, 2006.

Loos, Anita. *Kiss Hollywood Goodbye*. London: Virgin Books, 1974.

Moore, Susie. "How to Come Up with a Kick-Ass Personal Mantra." Greatist. March 8, 2016. http://greatist.com/live/mantras-how-to-create-a-mantra-for-personal-growth.

Stevenson, Robert Louis. *Lay Morals*. Amazon Digital Services, 2012.

Williams, Ray. "Do Self-Affirmations Work? A Revisit." *Psychology Today*. May 2013. https://www.psychologytoday.com/blog/wired-success/201305/do-self-affirmations-work-revisit.

Chapter 25: Friends

Kauffman, Jeffrey. "The Empathic Spirit in Grief Therapy." In *Techniques of Grief Therapy: Creative Practices for Counseling the Bereaved*, edited by Robert A. Neimeyer, 12–15. New York: Routledge, 2012.

Chapter 26: Creating Joy in Your Life after Tragedy

Dalai Lama, and Desmond Tutu. *The Book of Joy: Lasting Happiness in a Changing World*. With Douglas Abrams. New York: Avery, 2016.

Maude, Sara. "How to Create Joy Today: 7 Tips for a Happy Life." Tiny Buddha. http://tinybuddha.com/blog/how-to-create-joy-today-7-tips-for-a-happy-life/.

Chapter 27: Making It Through the Holidays

Miller, Linda. Personal letter used with permission.

Chapter 28: Finding a Therapist

"Find a Therapist." *Psychology Today.* https://therapists.psychologytoday.com.

"Find the Right Therapist." *GoodTherapy.org.* http://www.goodtherapy.org/find-therapist.html.

"How to Choose a Psychologist." *American Psychological Association.* http://www.apa.org/helpcenter/choose-therapist.aspx.

Lebow, Jay. L., Anthony L. Chambers, Andrew Christensen, and Susan M. Johnson. "Research on the Treatment of Couple Distress." *Journal of Marital and Family Therapy* 38, no. 1 (January 2012): 145–68. https://doi.org/10.1111/j.1752-0606.2011.00249.x.

Richo, David. *The Five Things We Cannot Change: And the Happiness We Find by Embracing Them.* Reprint ed. Boulder, CO: Shambhala Publications, 2006.

Smith, Melinda, and Jeanne Segal. "Finding a Therapist Who Can Help You Heal: Getting the Most out of Therapy and Counseling." *HelpGuide.org.* Last updated April 2018. http://www.helpguide.org/articles/emotional-health/finding-a-therapist-who-can-help-you-heal.htm.

Chapter 29: Group Work

"Coping with Loss: 115 Helpful Websites on Grief and Bereavement." *MastersInCounseling.org.* https://www.mastersincounseling.org/loss-grief-bereavement.html.

Cox, Patti. "Benefits of Grief Support Groups." *Hello Grief.* March 2014. http://www.hellogrief.org/benefits-of-grief-support-groups/.

"Grief Support Groups: Positives and Pitfalls." *What's Your Grief?* Last modified May 2, 2018. http://www.whatsyourgrief.com/grief-support-groups-positives-and-pitfalls/.

Paturel, Amy. "Power in Numbers: Research Is Pinpointing the Factors That Make Group Therapy Successful." *American Psychological Association.* November 2012. http://www.apa.org/monitor/2012/11/power.aspx/.

Wolfelt, Alan D. "Growing Through Grief: The Role of Support Groups." *GriefWords.com.* http://griefwords.com.

Chapter 30: Gratitude

Emmons, Robert A., and Michael E. McCullough. 2003. "Counting Blessings Versus Burdens: An Experimental Investigation of Gratitude and Subjective Well-Being in Daily Life." *Journal of Personality and Social Psychology* 84, no. 2 (February 2003): 377–89. 10. 1037/0022-3514.84.2.377.

King, Martin Luther Jr. *A Testament of Hope: The Essential Writings and Speeches.* Edited by James M. Washington. HarperOne reprint ed. New York: HarperOne, 2003.

Thoreau, Henry David. *Walden and Other Writings.* Reissue ed. New York: Bantam Books, 1983.

Chapter 31: Self-Compassion

Germer, Christopher K. *The Mindful Path to Self-Compassion.* New York: Guilford, 2009.

Neff, Kristin. *Self-Compassion*. New York: HarperCollins, 2011.

Neff, Kristin. "Self-Compassion Guided Meditations and Exercises." *Self-Compassion .org*. http://self-compassion.org/category/exercises/.

Chapter 32: Finding Peace Amid Political Turmoil

Campos, Gabriela. "Underlying Causes of Insecurity in Afghanistan." Edited by Erik Leaver. *Foreign Policy in Focus*. November 6, 2009. http://fpif.org/underlying_causes_of_insecurity_in_afghanistan/.

Esdaile, Charles. *Napoleon's Wars: An International History 1803–1815*. New York: Viking Penguin, 2008.

Freud, Sigmund. *Civilization and Its Discontents*. Reprint ed. New York: W. W. Norton, 2010.

Henderson, Nicole J., Christopher W. Ortiz, Naomi F. Sugie, and Joel Miller. *Law Enforcement and Arab American Community Relations After September 11, 2001: Technical Report*. New York: Vera Institute of Justice, 2006.

Joyce, James, quoted in Jack Sachs, comp., *The Book of Blessings*. Kennebunkport, ME: Cider Mill Press, 2006.

Krogstad, Jens Manuel, Jeffrey S. Passel, and D'Vera Cohn. "5 Facts About Illegal Immigration in the U.S." *Pew Research Center*. April 27, 2017. http://www .pewresearch.org/fact-tank/2016/11/03/5-facts-about-illegal-immigration-in-the-u-s/.

McLynn, Frank. *Genghis Kahn: His Conquests, His Empire, His Legacy*. Reprint ed. Boston: Da Capo, 2016.

Odidi, Godday. "The Problems, Challenges and Solutions to Insecurity in Nigeria." *The Nigerian Voice*. May 2, 2014. https://www.thenigerianvoice.com/news/ 144464/1/the-problems-challenges-and-solutions-to-insecurit.html.

Chapter 33: A Quick Pickup

Ahmad, S., A. Tejuja, K. D. Newman, R. Zarychanski, A. J. Seely. "Clinical Review: A Review and Analysis of Heart Rate Variability and the Diagnosis and Prognosis of Infection." *Critical Care* 13, no. 6 (2009): 232. 10.1186/cc8132.

Brown, R. P., and P.L. Gerberg. "Sudarshan Kriya Yogic Breathing in the Treatment of Stress, Anxiety, and Depression: Part I—Neurophysiologic Model." *Journal of Alternative and Complementary Medicine* 11, no. 1 (2005): 189–201. 11 189–201 10.1089/acm.2005.11.189.

Carter, Christine. "Greater Happiness in 5 Minutes a Day: How to Teach Kids Loving-Kindness Meditation." *Greater Good Magazine*. September 10, 2012. http://greatergood.berkeley.edu/raising_happiness/post/better_than_sex_and_ appropriate_for_kids.

Hanson, Rick. *Hardwiring Happiness: The New Brain Science of Contentment, Calm, and Confidence*. New York: Harmony Books, 2013.

Hatfield, Elaine, John T. Cacioppo, and Richard L. Rapson. "Primitive emotional contagion." In *Review of Personality and Social Psychology, Vol. 14 Emotion and Social Behavior*, edited by Margaret S. Clark, 151–77. Thousand Oaks, CA: Sage Publications, 1992.

Seaward, Brian Luke. *Managing Stress: Principles and Strategies for Health and Well-Being*. Sudbury, MA: Jones and Bartlett Learning, 2009.

Chapter 34: My Spirituality

Groen, Janet, Diana Coholic, John R. Graham, eds. *Spirituality in Social Work and Education: Theory, Practice, and Pedagogies*. Waterloo, ON: Wilfrid Laurier University Press, 2012.

Jung, Carl Gustav. *Psychology and Religion*. Reprint ed. New Haven, CT: Yale University Press, 1960.

Key, Kimberly. "A Spiritual Solution to Grief, Recovery and Free Will." *Psychology Today*. August 31, 2012. https://www.psychologytoday.com/blog/counseling-keys/201208/spiritual-solution-grief-recovery-free-will.

Kushner, Harold S. *When Bad Things Happen to Good People*. Reprint ed. New York: Knopf Doubleday, 2004.

Lewis, C. S. *A Grief Observed*. New York: HarperOne, 2001.

Lewis, C. S. *Mere Christianity*. Revised and enlarged ed. New York: HarperOne, 2015.

Wolfelt, Alan D. "The Spiritual Path to Healing: An Introduction." *GriefWords.com*. http://griefwords.com.

Acknowledgments

Thanks to my family for their unfailing love and encouragement. My critique group keeps me going: Margot Hovley, Shanna Hovley, Marion Jensen, Cory Webb, Jeanette Wright, Ken Lee, Scott Taylor, Knight Taylor. I appreciate their support. Thanks also to Keith and Becky Guernsey for their insight and advice. To the families who shared their tragedies with me, I am grateful. They wished to remain anonymous, so I am accommodating their wishes.

About the Author

Christy Monson has an MS in Counseling Psychology and Marriage and Family Therapy from University of Nevada at Las Vegas. She established a successful counseling practice in Las Vegas, Nevada. She is presently teaching continuing education classes for Weber State University. She is a staff writer for *Ensign Magazine*.

Her books include:
Texting Through Time Series
Love, Hugs, and Hope: When Scary Things Happen
Becoming Free: A Woman's Guide to Internal Strength
Family Talk
Finding Peace in Times of Tragedy

Her Native American coming-of-age book, *Banished*, received a Utah Arts Council Award and the Marilyn Brown award for Western Literature.

Visit her at:
www.christymonson.com
www.christymonson.blogspot.com
www.facebook.com/christymonsonauthor
twitter.com@ChristyMonson

About Familius

Visit Our Website: www.familius.com

Join Our Family

There are lots of ways to connect with us! Subscribe to our newsletters at www.familius.com to receive uplifting daily inspiration, essays from our Pater Familius, a free ebook every month, and the first word on special discounts and Familius news.

Get Bulk Discounts

If you feel a few friends and family might benefit from what you've read, let us know and we'll be happy to provide you with quantity discounts. Simply email us at orders@familius.com.

Connect

Facebook: www.facebook.com/paterfamilius
Twitter: @familiustalk, @paterfamilius1
Pinterest: www.pinterest.com/familius
Instagram: @familiustalk

FAMILIUS

The most important work you ever do will
be within the walls of your own home.